**Praise for *Depression:***

If I were to recommend just one book to read on depression, it would be this. Writing with the empathy, intelligence and non-judgemental insight that we now expect from him, Dr Barry shows that he has not only listened very carefully to those who suffer from depression and understood their distress, but has spent much effort compiling a practical guide devoted to coping with, and recovering from, this distressing condition.

*Carole Miriam Hunt, Sunday Independent*

*Depression: A practical guide* is a mine of information and is essential reading for those suffering with depression and for their families.

*Professor Patricia Casey, Department of Psychiatry, University College Dublin*

The book is a delight to read, with real life examples gained from clinical experience as a GP and CBT therapist. It outlines numerous practical exercises and tips to help in the recovery process, and provides the scientific rationale in an easy to follow, natural and compelling way.

*Professor Catherine Harmer, Cognitive Neuroscience, University of Oxford*

Gently, Dr Harry Barry takes the reader by the hand and explains how depression affects people differently – and how to get better. With simply-explained, precise medical and neurological details, he helps the reader understand the whole picture. Every home, school, university and workplace should have a copy of this book. *Cathy Kelly, author and UNICEF ambassador*

*Depression: A practical guide* is a masterfully crafted book that is essential reading for every person touched by depression, and every clinician who treats them. Dr Barry's writing is simple and empathic and well suited for a reader struggling with depression-related cognitive difficulties, yet his advice and exercises are practical, well evidenced, and sure to be helpful. Every frequently asked question about depression is covered, from biological to psychological to social. The patient stories are spot on and will resonate with everyone. I will be recommending *Depression: A practical guide* to patients and families, as well as to health science and medical students and residents.

*Professor Raymond W. Lam, University of British Columbia*

This warm and empathic book provides a manual for those whose lives are touched by depression, whether directly or through living with a sufferer. It also provides insights of great value for those in the caring professions both into the nature of depression and the range of treatment options that can benefit patients.

*Professor Larry Culpepper, Professor of Family Medicine, Boston University*

Dr Barry has done medicine and mental health a great service by writing an authoritative yet accessible exposition on cutting-edge thinking relating to recovery from states of depression. More than a self-help manual and better than many textbooks, it occupies a unique place in practical explanation and guidance to those affected by depression and those who work with them. You won't be sorry if you apply his sound and elegantly presented advice.

*Dr Justin Brophy, Foundation President, The College of Psychiatrists of Ireland*

What a pleasant and amazing contrast to read Harry Barry's book, *Depression: A practical guide*! Throughout the book, you feel the author's incredible experience and compassion for people suffering from depression, acknowledging with great sensibility their distress and suffering! Harry Barry simply knows what depression is and what it means to the patient. Even more, if you read the book, 'it sucks you in' because of the inspired style of writing and the consistent way to simplify issues and encourage the person to act and overcome! What an immense resource also for me as a therapist!

Without doubt this is the best depression book on the market and it should become the standard reference for both patients and professionals.

*Professor Hans-Ulrich Wittchen, Institute of Clinical Psychology and Psychotherapy,*
*University of Technology Dresden*

# DEPRESSION

## A practical guide

## DR HARRY BARRY

### A Note to Readers

*This book was originally published in 2012 as part of the Flag series. In preparation for the launch of the series in the UK and abroad, I have taken the opportunity to refresh and update the whole series. I have updated therefore some parts of* Depression, *to include some new insights into this condition in what is an ever-changing field.*

*All names, occupations and other details used in this book are allegorical in nature.*

*This book is dedicated to Karl McCormack (1982–2011) and Robert Tiernan (1974–2010), and to their families, friends and loved ones who live with the pain.*

First published in 2012 by Liberties Press, Ireland
This revised and updated edition published in 2017 by Orion Spring,
an imprint of The Orion Publishing Group Ltd
Carmelite House, 50 Victoria Embankment
London EC4Y 0DZ

An Hachette UK Company

1 3 5 7 9 10 8 6 4 2

A CIP catalogue record for this book is
available from the British Library.

ISBN: 978 1 4091 7449 3

Typeset by Input Data Services Ltd, Somerset

Printed in Great Britain by CPI Group (UK) Ltd, Croydon, CR0 4YY

www.orionbooks.co.uk

ORION
SPRING

# CONTENTS

# OUT OF THE DARKNESS

Imagine that you are out hill walking and become separated from your companions. It is late in the afternoon and dusk is approaching. In your haste to catch up, you trip, tumble and twist your ankle. The pain is excruciating and you find it difficult to walk. The panic increases as you struggle to continue. Will night fall before you reach a place of safety? Will anyone realise that you have become lost and are in pain?

Soon the effort required to walk becomes too much. You end up finding a spot that gives some shelter, and curl into a ball. It grows dark. The air temperature falls, and your feeling of isolation grows.

Soon it is pitch black and the fear and terror that you have tried to suppress arrive. Your thoughts become increasingly hopeless. 'I am going to die out here on the mountain alone, in pain and in darkness. There is no hope. They will never find me.' You have no phone and no way of contacting those you love. 'It is so lonely out here. I don't want to die.'

Your logical mind tells you that if you hang on long enough, the long hours of night will give way to the dawn. Eventually the sun will reappear, and with it light and warmth. But your emotional mind has already given up. It will be too late: you will not survive the bleakness, cold, pain and isolation. You don't think about money or possessions, or about how successful or not you are in your career; rather, you think about those you love and how precious life is. You may even start to pray to whatever god you believe in – for there are no atheists in a fox-hole, as any soldier will tell you.

The reality is that in such a situation, without help, there is a real chance that some of us may not make it. We have to depend on our own reserves of energy and resilience. We also have to rely on others to notice that we are missing and to come to rescue us from our difficulties. In such dangerous terrain, we may well need a guide who knows the ground. They may appear in the middle of the night with a search party, bringing heat, light and food to help us survive the journey back to civilisation. Even with all of these, the journey may be painful and fraught with difficulty.

This is where so many with depression find themselves. They can relate to the darkness, cold, pain, bleakness and isolation – and the terror that they are truly lost and will never make it to the dawn. But above all it is the darkness that is so frightening for them. For many, this darkness is caused by the absence of love in their lives. It is not the love of others that is absent – rather, acceptance and love of themselves. Once the sunlight of love is hidden by despair, the darkness becomes absolute. Will we ever see the dawn, with its promise of warmth and light?

But out of the darkness comes the light. For the night leads to the dawn, and with it the promise of a new day filled with light, hope and, above all, love.

*Dr Harry Barry*

# INTRODUCTION

Depression is a worldwide condition and one that causes immense distress to countless individuals and families in every corner of the globe. Depression is the leading cause of disability worldwide in terms of total years lost to ill health. There have been enormous efforts put into research to try and explain just what is happening in our mind and brain during episodes of this condition and indeed the effects on our physical health. Modern neuroscience is helping slowly to uncover some of the mystery and yet there is still much to be discovered.

Yet despite it being so common and so distressing to many, depression remains an extremely controversial subject. There is still a deeply ingrained stigma worldwide to the word and indeed many who suffer from the condition feel themselves extremely stigmatized and often hide their condition. It is as if mental health is still two to three decades behind physical health in terms of our understanding. It can be likened to the stigma that would have been afforded to conditions like TB or even AIDS in the more recent past.

The origins of this stigma lie back in a time when mental health was handled appallingly with many patients ending up in long stay institutions and with a litany of dreadful procedures such as lobotomies being performed to make them more docile.

Thankfully those awful days are long behind us and our understanding of mental health and its intimate relationship with our brain and body is being increasingly researched and better understood, leading to the search for better forms of treatment.

But there are other controversies still raging about depression. Most of these have centred on the role of drug therapy in the management of this condition and whether such therapy is doing more harm than good. Most of these concerns have focussed in on whether these drugs increase our suicide risks, or are addictive or are simply placebos. Other issues include concerns about the 'medicalization of sadness' where many experts worry that we are are simply trying to numb the pain of life.

We have also seen an explosion in the number of therapists and alternative practictioners who feel that they will be able to assist the person in managing their depression.

In the middle of all this confusion and uncertainty the person who is going through the darkness of a bout of depression can often feel even more isolated and alone. They are surrounded by a cloud of confusion, misinformation, stigma and many do not know where to turn or who to trust.

I have been a family doctor for over three decades and travelled with countless patients along the road of emotional pain so inherent in this condition. I have also been privileged to meet different specialists in different parts of the world and discuss how different traditions and approaches are applied to help patients heal. Of interest to me was the commonality of how patients present and how all the approaches, however varied, had to overcome the same obstacles.

So, depression no matter what part of the world you live in, takes very similar paths. The symptoms are generally quite similar, the world of stigma is almost universal, the fear of the condition equally common and the consequences of not managing it well equally destructive.

One of the greatest difficulties for the person with depression is the negative effect it has on our cognitive brain. So, just as we most need our brain to be at its sharpest, as we try to cope with the condition, we often find it struggling the most. It also creates in our mind and brain a ruminatory pattern of thinking which can be very distressing. And one of the critical consequences of this form of thinking is that it convinces us that we are of no worth and that coming for any assistance for the condition is a waste of time.

In my previous books in the *Flag* series I dealt with this illness in detail, explaining the underlying neuroscience behind depression, the causes of the illness, and therapies that can be used to treat it. One constant request is for a simple yet practical guide for sufferers to use on the journey. Most of us picking up a book or manual on a particular illness are able to quickly scan it and extract the relevant data. For those with significant depression, however, this task is unfortunately not so simple. It can be incredibly difficult, when you are completely exhausted and struggling with poor concentration and short-term memory, to get the most out of such books. Many have wondered if a practical guide could be created, providing a step-by-step approach to simply surviving the bout in question. The idea is to help the person recognise and deal with their condition; then, when they are well, they can peruse the other books in the *Flag* series for more detailed insight and information.

'Survival' is the word that depression sufferers can relate to best, because major depression is a physical, as well as a psychological illness. It drains our energy reserves, so we struggle to survive from day to day. Many of those who are fortunate enough not to suffer from this condition fail to understand this. For some, the fight simply to keep functioning becomes too hard, and thoughts of ending the pain become overwhelming. In this book, I will try to enter into the mind of a person with depression and show what it is like to inhabit their world. We are going to follow a group of people on their survival journey back to mental health. We will listen to their cries from the heart as they struggle with every step on the way. Accompanying them will be Dr Bill, whom we met in *Toxic Stress*. He is going to set out a four-step survival kit for the group and answer their questions along the way.

Firstly, I am going to give a simple summary of what depression is, why we develop it, the main physical and psychological symptoms experienced by the sufferer, and the modern holistic treatment approach to the condition.

For some readers, even this may be too much to cope with. I would encourage these readers to move on to the next section and only return to this one when they are feeling better.

My main objective in this book is to reach out to those who are suffering from depression. Many others, including the countless loved ones who struggle to understand and cope with the person in difficulty, may find the approach helpful too. Too often, people misunderstand what depression is and what the world of the person with it is actually like. This creates pain and suffering in many relationships. Information is the key to breaking this impasse. Hopefully, by challenging common misconceptions about depression, loved ones can empathise and support those in difficulty. There are also many counsellors, psychotherapists, occupational health departments, employers, family doctors and nurses who may benefit from a better understanding of what it is like to live in the hidden emotional world of depression.

Some people who pick up this book will have spent months, and in some cases years, suffering in secret pain from depression. Many will feel that their lives are of no value, and that it is pointless to seek help. Some may feel ashamed and dread those close to them 'learning their secret'. How would others view them if they found out? As we will see later, such thoughts come from our emotional brain, which, in someone with depression, has gone into negative mode.

Others living in this hidden world of pain and exhaustion can see no way out. Men in particular, due to the way they are 'hard-wired', and as a result of social expectations, are least likely to come forward for help. As a result, they often find themselves getting deeper into trouble. In the cauldron of modern Ireland, with its numerous economic and social problems, there is an even greater risk of men in difficulty feeling overlooked and forgotten.

If you are in such pain and don't know how to deal with it, or where to go for help, I appeal to you to join us on the journey. See how our group overcome their difficulties and pain – and, in most cases, make a full recovery. This may give you the courage and strength to make that first step:

- Talk to someone close to you
- Ring a helpline (see numbers at back of book)
- Open up to your family doctor or trusted counsellor, teacher or friend

Remember, suicide may often seem like the only way to end the pain. But it leaves in its wake a maelstrom of pain and life-long suffering for those who are left behind.

I hope in this book to show that there is another way: please join me on the journey.

# PART ONE

The word 'depression' is regularly used by many of us in our everyday lives. This has led to confusion, as some describe it as an emotion and others as an illness.

Periods of feeling down, sad or low, are, like anxiety, innate to the human condition. All of us experience such periods, following bereavements of loved ones or beloved pets, the ending of relationships, major disappointments and losses, illnesses of ourselves or loved ones, or stressful periods in our lives. Such periods are usually of short duration, and we quickly 'bounce back' to our normal selves. I often refer to this as 'depression the emotion, spelt with a small "d"!'

This distinction is crucial: when many hear the term 'depression', this is what they assume we are discussing. Since most of us experience such feelings regularly during our lives, we can become dismissive of the term. Didn't we too feel 'depressed' and manage to 'snap out of it'!

In this book, we are going to be dealing with a much more significant condition or illness, called 'major depression', or MD. This is a debilitating physical and psychological illness which affects around 400,000 people in Ireland.

As we will see later, major depression impinges greatly on our emotional world. But it is the extent and severity of the physical and psychological symptoms associated with MD which separates it from depression the emotion.

In this section, we'll examine the key symptoms, causes, simple neuroscience changes, and management of major depression.

*If you are struggling with energy levels and concentration, try to pick out the main headings from this section and move on. Later, when you are feeling better, you may like to return to learn more.*

## Major Depression: What Is It?

Major Depression is a physical and psychological illness which affects between 10 and 15 percent of the population.

### What Are The Main Symptoms?
*The main symptoms can be broken down into psychological, cognitive and physical:*

*Psychological Symptoms*

- low mood (which has to be present for a minimum period of two weeks on a daily basis, but is often present for months or years)
- loss of self-esteem
- negative thinking
- lack of pleasure in normal life experiences
- suicide thoughts and plans

### Let's See How This Is Expressed By Some Sufferers

*Low Mood*
'I feel weighed down by hopelessness and sadness. It is a physical pain in my heart, and no one understands how terrible it feels.'

John, a nineteen-year-old undergraduate student, has developed depression on moving away from his family for the first time, to live in a flat in Dublin. He is successfully hiding it from his family and friends. Alcohol relieves the pain for short periods, but its embrace is fleeting and illusory.

*Loss Of Self-Esteem*
'I am ashamed of the weak, useless, boring, incompetent failure that I am.

People hate spending time with me.'

Carl, a twenty-four-year-old mechanic, whose quiet disposition and painful shyness has disguised his inner torment from those close to him. Depression visited him first at the age of seventeen and has been an unwelcome but frequent visitor ever since.

## Anxiety

'I am constantly on a high state of alertness and always feel under pressure. I cannot cope when something goes wrong. I sometimes feel panicky for no obvious reason.'

Peter, aged twenty-two, has successfully hidden how he feels for the previous three years.

## Lack Of Pleasure (Anhedonia)

'I can barely manage a smile any more. I'm sick of people telling me to "cheer up" or that "it can't be that bad". It is – and much worse than they can imagine.'

Paula, aged twenty-eight, was sexually abused at the age of nine and has had bouts of depression for the past five years.

## Negative Thinking

'I cannot wait till I am dead. Then I will be at peace; the loneliness and hurt will be gone. I cannot go on, not like this. I have often thought of trying to explain how I feel to those closest to me, to share the pain. But what would be the point? After all, there is nothing they or anyone else can do to help, and I would only be burdening them with my troubles.'

Andrew, a twenty-six-year-old postgraduate, is suffering from his second major bout of depression. Like many others with this illness, he is having relationship difficulties with his girlfriend, blaming her for not seeing his pain, and using alcohol in large quantities. This does little to silence his negative thoughts that he doesn't deserve to live: as he sees it, no one, including his girlfriend, would notice if he was gone.

*Suicide Thoughts*

'The world will be a much better place without me. I am a burden on everyone, and they won't miss me at all.'

Jack, who is twenty-nine, has already quietly planned in great detail how he will end the pain. If his depression is not recognised and remains untreated, he may soon put these thoughts into action. This is made more likely following his recent dramatic increase in alcohol consumption to numb the pain of a breakup with his girlfriend.

## Let's Examine These In More Detail

The low mood is not just having a bad day! It is like being in a dark hole or well with high walls all around, surrounded by darkness, with only a brief glimpse of light visible. One can see no way of climbing out. It is a world of deep-seated emotional pain, a shrivelling up of our very soul. Mothers have often described it as a pain more intense than labour. Others have described days with it as being seemingly endless, with no end to the arid wasteland within.

The lack of self-esteem goes to the very heart of how the person feels about themselves. They feel of no value and in some cases 'invisible'. They believe, erroneously, that they are a burden on those around them and not worth knowing or interacting with. This explains why many people with MD seemingly reject those closest to them, like family and friends. It is not that they are rejecting the latter, rather that they don't want to burden them with the worthless person they feel they have become.

The lack of pleasure can be partial or, in many cases, almost total. Many will derive no pleasure from normal human actions and interactions – such as food, sex and social interaction. Many describe being out socially in crowds and desperately trying to show interest or enjoyment in what is going on, but failing miserably. Many with MD will misuse alcohol in such situations, in order to conceal how they truly feel.

The anxiety experienced in MD is nearly always intermingled with exhaustion. Although the person may feel anxious, they are almost apathetic in relation to their condition. Some may present more acutely with panic attacks, while others may experience an agitated, restless form of anxiety, with both physical and mental symptoms (worrying).

Negative thinking is now known to lie at the heart of MD. People with depression start to view themselves, those around them and indeed the world itself through a dark lens. This black curtain around the person prevents them from seeking help. It is the source of much of the psychological pain and constant ruminations characteristic of this illness.

Suicide thoughts are common in MD. This knowledge is often a great relief for the person with this illness. Many cry with relief when asked: 'Are you, as so many with this condition do, having thoughts of self-harming?' They are often ashamed for having such thoughts. It is a weight off their shoulders to realise that it is common for people with depression to experience these thoughts. However, if one is actually to start to investigate, or 'plan', how to end it all, then matters become more serious. This is a strong indicator that we are becoming significantly depressed. It is a real cry for help from our emotional brain, and we must heed it and seek assistance.

*Physical Symptoms*

- Fatigue
- sleep difficulties
- weight loss or gain
- loss of drive (including sex drive)
- poor memory (both short-term and long-term)
- poor concentration

## Let's See How This Is Expressed By Some Sufferers
*Fatigue*

'The simplest of tasks drains me of all my energy; I just want to sleep all the time.'

Mary, a twenty-seven-year-old mother with two small children, has developed symptoms of depression following a series of stressful events, in particular the death of a close friend from cancer.

*Sleep Difficulties*

'I just can't seem to sleep through the night. I'm always so exhausted in the morning.'

Thomas, a thirty-two-year-old successful businessman, has been suffering from undiagnosed bouts of depression for more than a decade.

*Weight Loss Or Gain*

'I'm just not hungry any more. Food does not look appetising, and it's too much energy to eat. Hopefully I will waste away to nothing.'

Catherine, a single parent aged twenty-four. The stress of coping with a small child, while living on social welfare in a small, poorly equipped flat, with a partner who abuses alcohol (and her), has triggered a bout of depression. She has lost more than a stone in weight. Her diet (already poor due to lack of money and poor knowledge about nutrition) has been reduced to coffee and cigarettes.

Or:

'Eating has become a habit for me: it distracts me from how I feel for a while. Then I feel worse as I get fatter and uglier. But who is going to look twice at me anyway?'

Michael, who, although presenting an outer image of seeming normality, has suffered for years with poor self-esteem. Now, at the age of thirty, he is grossly obese from years of using food as a coping mechanism for his bouts of low mood.

*Loss Of Drive*

'I don't enjoy any of the activities that I used to. It all seems like so much effort now, and I don't see the point.'

Maura, a twenty-four-year-old working mother, developed depression three months after the birth of her first child.

*Cognitive Symptoms*

- poor memory

- reduced concentration
- indecisiveness and difficulties with problem solving

*Poor Memory*

'I have become increasingly forgetful, and have difficulty remembering the simplest of things, like what I did yesterday.'

Noreen, a single, very busy twenty-seven-year-old manager, is struggling to cope with her day-to-day duties due to depression triggered by a prolonged period of sustained stress.

*Reduced Concentration*

'I don't read any more. It is too much effort to make sense out of the words, and it is becoming difficult to pay attention to anything.'

George, a seventeen-year-old student, is struggling to study as he battles with a bout of unrecognised depression.

## Let's Examine These In More Detail

The fatigue described by most with MD is not the same as the fatigue experienced after a hard day of physical or mental work. It is a deep-seated state of exhaustion where even the simplest task becomes a major ordeal. It is actually a form of mental fatigue but will seem physical in nature to the person involved. As a result, they stop all forms of exercise, in the mistaken belief that this will conserve whatever energy remains. Fatigue intrudes into every area of their lives, making their life extremely difficult. This is another reason why sufferers from MD try to avoid social contact: as they see it, this will mean expending energy they simply do not have. Students with depression will often be thought to be lazy, as they can't study; employees may be felt to be not pulling their weight; and young men may cut themselves off from friends and stop taking part in sports – all due to this debilitating fatigue.

The sleep difficulties so common in MD come from biological changes to sleep rhythms and in particular our dream sleep (often called 'REM sleep'). Normally we sleep for around eight hours per night. When we are well, we do most of our dreaming in the second part of the night. But in MD, this pattern is turned back to front, so we find ourselves waking up in the early hours of the morning and struggling to get back to sleep. Sleep in depression is nearly always a problem: it is difficult to fall asleep, and to stay asleep. The result is that many feel exhausted when they rise in the morning, and wonder how to face the day.

The weight loss/gain in depression comes from the fact that we may lose interest in food, as we get no buzz or enjoyment from it. Or we may find ourselves eating all the wrong kinds of food in a desperate attempt to try to lift our mood. The weight loss in particular is a warning sign that something is wrong. Many assume that the only reason we can lose weight is if we either have a serious underlying physical illness or an eating disorder. This is an obvious physical symptom that might tip off either the person with MD or those around them that something is awry. In the case of young men, this may be the only visible warning sign.

Loss of drive is another significant physical symptom that may dominate the life of the person with MD. All of us have innate drive, which gives us interest and enthusiasm to carry out normal human daily activities. As a result we eat, have sex and involve ourselves in work and hobbies. In depression, this drive dries up and we lose interest in food, sex, work and hobbies. Our lives become arid, and nothing matters. The loss of libido, or sex drive, causes further difficulties within relationships, as the partner involved (unless they have some understanding of MD) feels rejected and unloved. In fact, the illness, and not the people involved, is driving this loss of libido. This loss of drive also explains a seeming lack of enthusiasm to take on new challenges at work.

Poor memory is another physical symptom which causes problems. In depression, the memory part of our brain is physically attacked. MD interferes with the production and retrieval of both short-term and longer-term memory. Many who do not understand this illness fail to grasp that this inability to retain even simple, short-term memories can be quite profound. As a result, it can be difficult in some cases to deal with depression using talk therapies alone: the person may struggle to retain the information discussed. This memory difficulty can make it hard for a housewife to carry out her normal shopping and other chores, for example, or for students to study for exams.

It also explains why some people with MD forget appointments and dates – something which can interfere with their working and social lives.

Reduced concentration goes hand in hand with the memory difficulties discussed above. Most of us take for granted the capacity to focus on and retain information. The simplest example of this is reading the daily newspaper – something we do without difficulty. In depression, however, the words become a blur. Many will talk about picking up the paper and reading the words, but being unable to put them together, and eventually putting the paper down, frustrated. This loss of concentration is a particular for students, who may be unable to focus on and retain the information contained in books and manuals. Once again, this may be construed as laziness; in reality, it is a result of MD.

Indecisiveness and difficulties with problem solving are common symptoms which can cause significant difficulties. These are often called executive function difficulties, where during a bout of major depression, parts of our logical brain are really struggling to make normal everyday decisions. This once again can cause chaos in our working, academic and domestic lives.

To be diagnosed with MD, one must have significantly depressed mood for more than two weeks, combined with at least four of the above additional symptoms, particularly difficulties with sleep, appetite or fatigue, feelings of worthlessness, suicide thoughts and a loss of enjoyment of life. In practice, most people will have the majority of above-mentioned symptoms. If one can imagine living in a world where these are present in our lives day after day, month after month – in a seemingly endless round – then we can visualise major depression!

## Major Depression:
## What Is Happening In The Brain And Body?

I am going to keep neuroscientific information to simple key concepts, and refer those who wish to know more to my other books.

We all have a logical and an emotional brain. The logical brain:

- is called the 'prefrontal cortex' and is situated at the front of the brain

- makes up 29 percent of the brain
- is the rational, logical, problem-solving part of the brain
- helps us be creative, analytical and capable of planning
- controls emotions and behaviour, particularly impulsive, self-destructive behaviour
- controls social relationships and empathy.

The emotional brain:

- is called the 'limbic system' and is situated in the middle of the brain
- controls our stress system
- is involved in the processing of emotions (particularly negative ones such as anxiety and depression)
- is involved in the creation, storage and retrieval of memories
- is involved in the enjoyment of food, sex and alcohol

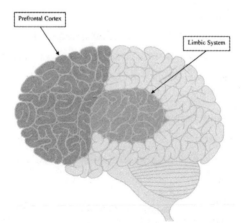

*Figure 1: The logical and emotional brain*

A key player in the emotional brain that is felt to be at the heart of depression and indeed all forms of anxiety is called the amygdala. It is not necessary to know much about this little organ present on both sides of our brain, other than that it oversees our stress system and is the generator of emotions such as sadness, anxiety and anger. It also stores the memory of these emotions.

One of the most consistent findings on Neuroimaging is that when a person with major depression is exposed to a negative image, the amygdala is consistently overactive. The amygdala is part of an over active circuit seen as the generator of most of the symptoms of major depression. For the rest of this discussion we will simply however regard the emotional brain as a single unit. Our emotional brain is also much faster and not as nuanced as our more rational prefrontal cortex which is slower and more measured in its opinions and actions. It can be compared to the accelerator and brake in a car. The prefrontal cortex is the brake whilst the limbic system or emotional brain is the accelerator. Many assume that our logical brain is more powerful than our emotional brain. In practice, however, there are more connections and pathways running from the emotional brain to the logical brain than the reverse. Daily decisions are made with emotion and logic combined, with emotion playing the greater role (with a split of around 60/40).

When we are well, our emotions and logic are in harmony. So when we are undergoing typical everyday highs and lows, our logical brain has the ability to 'keep manners on' our more disobedient emotional brain. The logical brain is the protective mechanism our body and brain uses to keep us grounded.

When we are unwell, negative emotions overwhelm our logical brain; the classic example of this is major depression. At its most simple, this is a breakdown in the normal balance between our logical and emotional brain. This results in our logical brain being unable to switch off the torrent of negative thoughts and emotions flowing from our emotional brain. There is quite a complex neurocircuitry between our more rational prefrontal cortex and our more emotional limbic system. It is a breakdown, in the normal flow through this neurocircuitry, that results in depression.

If we grasp this simple concept, then it becomes much easier to understand the illness of depression. This breakdown gives rise to most of the psychological symptoms of MD.

To understand many of the physical symptoms of MD, we need to realise that our emotional and logical brains are connected by three mood cables (which operate like simple telephone lines between the two). These are:

- the SEROTONIN CABLE, involved in mood, sex, sleep, appetite, memory and impulsive behaviour (including self-harm and suicide)
- the NORADRENALIN CABLE, involved in energy, sleep, drive and concentration
- the DOPAMINE CABLE, involved in our sense of enjoyment of food, sex and anything else that gives us pleasure

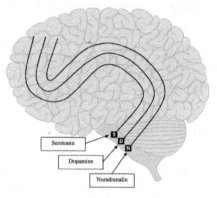

*Figure 2: The three mood cables*

When we develop MD, these three mood cables become underactive, producing the following symptoms:

- Reduced activity in the serotonin mood cable leads to low mood; sleep, sex and appetite difficulties; an increase in anxiety; and an increase in suicide thoughts and impulsive behaviour.
- Reduced activity in the noradrenalin mood cable leads to poor drive and concentration, fatigue and sleep difficulties.
- Reduced activity in the dopamine mood cable leads to a reduction in enjoyment of life, particularly in relation to food and sex, and an overreliance on stimulants like alcohol.

The last link in the chain is that our emotional brain takes charge of our stress system. It does so by controlling the adrenal stress gland, situated one on each side of the abdomen over our kidneys, and by the main stress hormone produced by this gland, called glucocortisol.

We now know that in MD, the emotional brain sends the stress system into overdrive creating the following symptoms:

- The adrenalin stress gland is overactive in depression, occasionally doubling in size.
- The stress hormone glucocortisol is elevated, both during the day and, in particular, at night time.
- This leads to an increased risk of significant physical problems namely heart disease and stroke (sticky platelets), osteoporosis, infections and diabetes, among other things.

In summary, this is what happens in MD:

- The emotional brain, triggered by stress, goes into negative mode.
- There is a breakdown in the normal ability of the logical brain to switch off the emotional brain.
- As a result, the emotional brain causes the stress system to become overactive, producing too much glucocortisol.
- The stress system attacks the three mood cables, which become underactive.
- The whole host of physical and psychological symptoms of this illness follow.

But why do we experience such an absence of pleasure and joy in our lives when depressed and why do we struggle so much with memory? These are two important questons.

We now know that the left side of our brain is very important for positive emotions like joy and the right side is much more focused on negative emotions such as depression and anxiety. One part of our emotional brain on the left side is called the Nucleus Accumbens which is where we experience feelings of pleasure. In MD, this is often underactive giving rise to the lack of joy in our lives during a bout.

There is a second key section in our emotional brain which organizes our whole world of contextual memories called the Hippocampus. This becomes impaired due to high levels of our stress hormones in depression leading to our difficulties in this area.

If you are reading this and are struggling with concentration, don't worry. Take one main thought from this section: MD is caused by a breakdown in the ability of our logical brain to switch off our negative emotional brain. In fact, this is the key to the whole book. Now move on and return to this section later, when you are feeling better.

## What Is The Role Of 'Hot' And 'Cold' Cognition In Major Depression?

Increasingly research is focusing on the role of cognition and its role in depression. We have always known that concentration was a significant issue for many during a bout of depression. But we are beginning to understand that cognitive difficulties are much more extensive than previously thought.

Cognition can be described as 'hot' or 'cold'.

Hot cognition relates to the way our thinking is influenced by our emotions. So, in depression we are more biased towards paying attention to the negative in our environment. We also tend to be excessively influenced by any form of perceived negative feedback from others. Finally, we are inclined to be biased towards increased memory for negative cues.

Cold cognition relates to cognitive processes independent of emotional involvement. So, it relates more to cognitive functions such as attention, memory and decision making.

In depression, both occur regularly during a bout. Whilst we have always been aware of hot cognition there has been an increasing interest in cold cognition.

If for example I believe in MD that 'I am worthless' then this thought becomes linked to the emotion of depression, then I have triggered a hot cognitive thought. This is an example of hot cognition.

Whereas if during a bout, I find myself struggling with memory, attention, concentration, and other key functions such as decision making then my cold cognition has become impaired. It is now accepted that over ninety percent of those suffering a bout of MD will be experiencing such cold cognitive difficulties.

This is important for students for example who may find themselves struggling with absorbing and retaining information from lectures and quickly fall behind. Or for both workers and managerial staff who if suffering from such difficulties may struggle to hold down their jobs. This is a common cause of absenteeism and presentism in the workplace.

In practice, hot and cold cognitive difficulties feed on one another in depression. If I struggle to carry out normal tasks due to cold cognitive difficulties then I end up rating myself as worthless, triggering a further drop in mood.

Of some concern is the finding that some who have recovered from a bout of depression may still have some lingering cold cognitive difficulties.

These hot and cold cognitive difficulties in depression are all created by neurocircuitry malfunctioning in our emotional and logical brain.

## Major Depression: Why Do We Get It At All?

There has been an explosion in our understanding of MD in the past ten years. This has been driven by our new understanding of the brain. In particular, information is emerging on how the brain develops and interacts with our environment at all stages of life.

The crucial links between the emotional and logical brain, described above, can be disrupted due to the following:

- the genes we inherit from our parents
- being exposed environmentally to a family pattern of depression or anxiety
- significant stressors in our early childhood and adolescence (these include abuse in any form, coming from an addictive or non-validating family environment, bullying, sexual-identity issues, being overprotected as we are growing, and poverty)
- sex hormones, particularly in women (oestrogen and progesterone)
- exposure to high levels of stress from everyday life

- the deleterious effects of alcohol and drugs, particularly in our youth and old age
- vascular changes in the brain as we age

Current thinking is that many who will later develop MD, through a combination of genes and the environmental influences described above, are predisposed to not handling chronic stress as well as other people. This may be because key pathways between emotional and logical brain have been affected during childhood and adolescence. This can make it more difficult for the logical brain to control the emotional brain when it turns negative.

When life throws up significant stressors, such as loss, relationship difficulties, pregnancy and the postnatal period, sexual-identity issues, financial problems and so on, the underlying predisposition is exposed, and our emotional brain dives into a negative, depression mode. When this happens, the normal control of the logical brain is impaired, and the logical brain becomes swamped by the negative barrage emanating from the emotional brain.

If this happens on a number of occasions, it takes less and less stress for the emotional brain to trigger future episodes, until, eventually, simple negative thinking can start an episode. Some researchers assume that MD is primarily caused by our genes; others that it is purely environmental in nature. In practice, it is a balance between the two. The stronger the familial incidence of MD, the more at risk we are of developing it. But there will usually be some environmental triggers which activate the relevant genes.

## Is Depression A Dietary Illness?

Some experts wonder whether a lack of important proteins, fats and vitamins in our daily lives may explain fully the mystery of depression. Renowned nutritionist Patrick Holford is a leading advocate of this possibility. While I feel that the absence of such nutrients from a person's diet may play a role in the expression and severity of depression, it is highly unlikely that this is the full story. Genetic predispositions and other environmental influences, particularly those which trigger stress, play a larger part in this illness than nutrition.

## When Does MD Appear First, And How Long Do Episodes Last?

While children under twelve occasionally suffer from MD, in general it seems to occur from puberty onwards. Depression can appear at any stage of a person's life, but often occurs for the first time before the age of thirty, and frequently following periods of great stress. Twenty-five percent of sufferers will first show signs of the illness during their teens. This group is more likely to become chronically depressed and prone to relapse. Others will develop depression later, either postnatally or following a major stress incident, such as loss of a loved one or the ending of a key relationship.

Episodes can vary greatly in duration but the average period is six to twelve months. For those affected, this can seem like an eternity. Usually the depression will begin to lift after this period but some will experience chronic or persistent symptoms.

## Why Do Bouts Of MD Eventually Subside?

We know that most of those who experience a bout of MD will, even without any treatment, eventually seem to get better. The duration of time this will takes can vary from six to twelve months. This question is one of many questions about this illness that we struggle to answer with certainty.

The current opinion is that the brain does not like any imbalance and prefers the world of homeostasis which can be best defined as 'business as usual'! It therefore is desperately trying to restore this normal balance of power between the logical and emotional brain. It eventually begins to win this battle over time and most of the symptoms begin to gradually recede.

This may of course be assisted if the stressors that may have triggered the episode are resolved and the person is under less stress.

We do know however that if bouts are significant and not managed properly it seems as if the brain remains extremely vulnerable to future episodes and often within a year or two. The opposite also pertains. There is increasing evidence that recognizing and treating particularly first episodes earlier and aggressively may significantly reduce further episodes.

## How Often Will An Individual Suffer A Bout Of Depression?

It is estimated that 75 percent of those who suffer from a significant bout of depression will undergo between one and four depressive episodes in their lifetime. In 75 percent of cases, there will be another episode of this illness within five years of the first one.

It is also believed (probably for biological as well as psychological reasons) that each episode makes further ones more likely, particularly if the condition is not treated.

These bouts often occur after a period of significant stress. This is why it is particularly important for people with depression to develop coping mechanisms to deal with stress.

The remaining 25 percent will experience constant bouts of low mood, alternating with periods of feeling relatively 'normal'. In this group, the depression is likely to start in the teenage years, and often needs only the most apparently minor of stress triggers to reactivate it.

## Why Is MD More Common In Women?

We know that women are twice as likely as men to develop major depression. Many theories have been put forward as to why this is the case. These include the following:

- The serotonin mood cable is 50 percent less active in women than in men. Since this cable is a key player in depression and anxiety, this may predispose women to these conditions.
- Women are exposed to significant hormonal shifts during their lives – much more so than men – as witnessed by the incidence of postnatal depression in women.
- Women experience more stress in their lives. This may in part occur because of the fact that they generally play a larger role in rearing children and looking after elderly parents than men.
- There are significant differences between the male and female brains, in terms of both hard-wiring and functioning. Women, for example, are

multi-taskers, whereas men find it easier to concentrate on single tasks. This may put more stress on women as a result.

- In a world where women have been encouraged to go out into the workforce as well as carrying out domestic responsibilities, there is a risk of the stress involved in juggling these different roles triggering bouts of depression.
- There is recent evidence that biologically when stressed women have a different mechanism for handling their stress hormone Glucocortisol that puts them at greater risk from stress.
- There may be a difference in genetic predisposition to MD between men and women. Until we have learnt more about the genes involved, we will have to wait and see if this is the case.

## Is Major Depression Just A Single Entity?

For many decades, MD, has been considered by professionals and lay people as being a single entity. But increasingly as we learn more about this illness it is becoming clearer that this may not be the case. So, we are now recognizing that some sufferers will complain of significant levels of anhedonia for example and so struggle during episodes from a profound loss of enjoyment in their lives.

Others may not suffer from anhedonia but may suffer from profound apathy or lack of motivation. Others may have profound cognitive difficulties with attention and concentration and others less so. Others may have a lot of the psychological symptoms and fewer physical ones; and vice versa.

Increasingly there is a belief that over time we will redefine depression into sub groups with emphasis on the main symptoms pertinent to each individual person.

We may eventually even be able to explain why these differences occur and more importantly may be better able to tailor treatment options for each person individually. We may be better able to decide on whether one person might do better with talk therapies such as CBT and others may require more drug therapy. And in the case of the latter it may inform us better as to which one should be used on an individual basis.

For simplicity in this book we are going to treat it as a homogenous unit.

## Can We Think Our Way Into Or Out Of A Bout Of Major Depression?

Increasingly we are becoming more aware of the power of the mind to reshape the brain. So, can we simply think our way into a bout of major depression? For if this were the case it would assume that we could in turn think our way out of a bout.

We have already mentioned rumination (the washing machine of negative thoughts in your head) which is a form of thinking very prevalent in major depression. But this seems to be part of a general slide of the emotional brain into negativity where we assign a negative bias to everything we encounter when depressed. We search the environment only for evidence that this irrational way of looking at the world is true and ignore all else.

We also know that challenging this form of thinking is critical to assisting a person not only to emerge from a bout of MD but in reducing their chances of a recurrence.

The usual pattern of depression is that the first few episodes follow on from some stressful triggers that we are struggling to cope with. This seems to trigger the emotional brain to become more negative. It also fires up our stress system. Eventually the capacity of our logical brain to calm down the emotional brain becomes swamped and the full spectrum of symptoms arise. As part of that package our thinking becomes very negative and ruminatory.

But we do know that eventually for some people the levels of stress that are needed to trigger a further bout seem to decrease until for some a slide into negative ruminatory thinking can be enough to trigger it. This is because persistent bouts damage the neurocircuitry control mechanisms of the logical brain over the emotional brain further. This explains why, as we will examine later, CBT type approaches to tackling our negative thinking can be so vital.

In terms of thinking our way out of a bout, as any sufferer will attest, it is not quite so easy! You can't just think your way out of a bout. We do know however that the mind is a powerful tool at our disposal to manage a bout of depression but only as part of a structured, organized holistic package, where we develop techniques to harness this power.

Part of the difficulty is that quite often during a bout of depression our emotional brain is so distressed that the more rational part of our brain is simply not able to calm it down. This is worsened by the cognitive difficulties involving attention, concentration and memory. We will be discussing this in more detail later.

One potential area of interest for the future lies in trying to pre-empt the first bout of depression in younger age groups by trying to identify negative thinking pattens that can be triggered by stress and perhaps building into our educational system skills to reshape them.

## What Is Late Onset Depression?

It is important to distinguish between early onset depression where the first bout occurs earlier in our lives – usually starting between fifteen and thirty-five – and late onset depression which usually starts over the age of fifty.

Late onset depression, as the name suggests, is where we experience our first bout of depression over the age of sixty in the UK. Often the person has had no experience of low mood or depression and then suddenly begins to develop the typical symptoms as they are getting older.

The symptoms can be extremely distressing for both the person and their families. They are once again a mixture of psychological, cognitive and physical.

They may include:

- Extremely sad and low mood – at the bottom of a dark well with no way of ever finding oneself back in the light again.
- Marked lack of enjoyment for anything in life – joy is sucked out of life – what is the point of existence.
- Marked lack of interest in all aspects of our lives.
- Significant insomnia.
- Loss of appetite and weight loss.
- Fatigue – struggling to get through each day.
- Psychomotor retardation – where my body will simply not do what my mind wants it to do at the same speed as normal
- Constant anxiety about physical symptoms.
- Major difficulties with cognition – in memory, concentration, decision making and problem solving.

- Hopelessness and complete negativity about the future.
- Constant ruminations often filled with emotions of guilt, anxiety and depression.
- Profound sense of worthlessness.
- Significant thoughts of and sometimes serious planning about suicide (the predominant risk factor for suicide in late life is depression, which is present in approximately 85% of older adults who died by suicide).

The causes are varied but the majority are more likely to have cererbrovascular changes in the brain which increase our vulnerability to major depression by disrupting circuits between our emotional and logical brains. This occurs because atherosclerotic changes in small arteries which supply the neurocircuitry reduce blood supply to it. We can also develop significant late onset depression after a significant stroke affecting the left side of brain for similar reasons. Other illnesses such as Parkinson's Disease can also be a trigger. It can also on occasions be associated with latent dementia.

The good news is that once again a sensible holistic therapy package can assist us in dealing with such a bout.

## The Dynamic Nature Of Our Brain And Its Capacity To Change

Before we proceed to see how MD is best treated we will just briefly discuss the capacity of the brain to change which we call Neuroplasticity. This means that from birth to death our brain is constantly and dramatically reshaping itself all the time. One of the most powerful energy sources that can assist this process is our own mind. It is one of the mysteries of life that our mind which is partly created by our brain can be an energy source available to reshape the brain! So how we think can have a profound effect on brain pathways.

This is a key concept as it lies at the heart of our management of bouts of MD. All therapies whether they be lifestyle change such as exercise, talk therapies such as CBT or indeed drug therapy or alternative therapies have the capacity to change or reshape our brain pathways and circuits to counter the signs and symptoms of depression.

For those who would like to examine these concepts in detail, I will refer them to one of my books *Flagging the Therapy*.

One of the most powerful triggers for change can be empathy. So, lets examine how empathy and other therapies can assist us in recovering from a bout.

## How Can MD Be Treated?

The most important message is that MD is a completely treatable condition. After decades of confusion and uncertainty as to how it should be managed, a modern holistic approach to MD is emerging. Modern neuroscience has assisted us greatly in showing that all therapies act on common pathways in the brain. For those who would like to examine this in detail, I will refer them to my first two books, *Flagging the Problem* and *Flagging the Therapy*.

Here is a simple summary of the holistic approach. The 'holistic pyramid' is composed of a solid foundation of empathy and lifestyle changes; on top of this, we add talk and drug therapies.

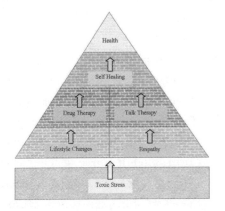

*Figure 3: The holistic therapy pyramid*

### What Is Empathy?
The ability to sense where another person 'is' emotionally is called empathy. Everyone possesses this innate ability, but they may not recognise it. We use this skill in everyday human interactions without thinking about it. When in

distress, just as when you are depressed, you must be careful to choose somebody with whom you feel an empathy bond. You must sense that there is a 'meeting of minds', and that you are comfortable to 'open up' to the world of pain and darkness you are experiencing.

Some may have this bond with their family doctor, others with a therapist or counsellor, a psychiatrist or psychologist, a family member or close friend, or a spiritual advisor.

For many with depression, this is often the first, most important, but most difficult step of all. Later, we will examine typical thoughts that stop this bond developing.

## What Are The Main Lifestyle Changes Needed To Combat MD?

Because of the tendency among psychologists/therapists to emphasise the psychological rather than the physical nature of major depression, lifestyle changes are often overlooked. Yet their role in treating MD is crucial. Let's examine the key ones:

### Exercise

Simple exercise is one of the most powerful tools at our disposal to both treat and prevent relapses of major depression, and research is increasingly supporting this viewpoint. Constant, regular exercise positively regulates cognitive functions, mood, motivation, memory, the ability to cope with stress, and the ability to plan and problem-solve. It helps lift depression, reduces feelings of helplessness and alleviates anxiety. Exercise also improves interest and drive – things which are often lacking in people experiencing depression.

What form of exercise is most beneficial, how often and for how long, are questions that are currently exercising top research minds. The following is the general consensus:

- Thirty minutes of brisk exercise, preferably three to five times a week, is ideal.
- Exercising for longer periods does not confer extra benefits.
- If walking, it is advisable to do so in the fresh air, due to the beneficial

effects of sunlight, an important source of vitamin D.

- Any form of exercise is beneficial, from walking and jogging to weightlifting and swimming.
- Creative exercise, like dancing and water aerobics, is equally effective and provides an extra social dimension.
- If there are difficulties with motivation, it is worth building up to the above ideal situation in small daily increments.

There are less obvious mental health benefits to regular exercise, mainly in the social/empathy areas. Many people with depression lose interest in meeting other people due to fatigue and lack of enjoyment. If they interact socially during walking, jogging, dancing, swimming or going to the gym, this can only be positive.

In short, exercise is the simplest and most powerful lifestyle therapeutic tool at our disposal.

## Nutrition

There is a huge amount of interest in this subject, as a visit to any bookshop will verify, with many claims relating to nutrition being made in relation to the treatment of depression in particular. There is a clear place for proper nutrition as part of an overall treatment package, but too many claims have not been scientifically validated. I counsel a healthy dose of common sense when reading much of the dietary-related health literature out there. Having reviewed the research, I recommend the following:

- A sensible mix of fresh fish (particularly oily fish like salmon, mackerel and tuna), eggs (especially freerange ones), meat, vegetables, cereals, nuts, flax seed and oils, grains and fruit.
- Prepare your own food whenever possible, and avoid fast food and highly processed packaged food.
- Eat – even if, when depressed, you can't see any point or pleasure in the task – as our brain cannot run without fuel.
- Avoid high-stimulant drinks like coffee and Coke, which many with

depression and anxiety use in abundance.

- Avoid high-sugar 'hits', as having dramatically fluctuating blood-sugar levels is not helpful to brain functioning.
- Avoid the extreme diets sometimes recommended by alternative 'experts', as these often exclude key nutrients and supplements.
- Avoid using food as a 'crutch' when feeling down or anxious; at the same time, remember that starving the brain of vital nutrition, as often happens in depression, is equally damaging.
- In the area of supplements, the main ones that are generally believed to play a role in enhancing mental health are Omega 3 fish oils, and the key B vitamins folic acid, B6 and B12. All of these have been extensively investigated and there is substantial evidence to support their use as part of a holistic package, particularly in depression.
- I recommend a B-complex supplement daily and Omega 3 oils (particularly EPA), in a dose of 500-1000 mgs for those with a history of depression.

## The Role Of Alcohol And Other Drugs

It may seem unusual to include alcohol and illegal substances like hash, cocaine and ecstasy in a discussion on the treatment of depression, but dealing with the misuse and abuse of these substances is of great importance. The developing brain is extremely sensitive to alcohol and the above-named drugs; adult brain pathways are not fully formed until the age of twenty-five to thirty. Misuse of alcohol is almost endemic in the twelve- to-thirty age group, so these pathways are open to being disrupted – increasing the risks of illnesses like depression. Misuse of hash and cocaine, though less common, is prevalent and equally disruptive, increasing risks of psychosis and depression.

There is particular concern about their use among those under the age of fifteen.

When depressed as teenagers or adults, we may use alcohol or drugs to treat associated emotional and physical symptoms. This sets up a vicious circle: depression causes low mood, alcohol (a depressant) is used to lift it, causing a further drop in mood, and so on. It can be difficult to treat depression without breaking this pattern.

The use of illegal drugs has to permanently cease, otherwise all therapies will struggle to have an effect. I have seen some people transform their lives by facing their 'demons' in this area. It is particularly important for young people to take this step, as their brains are particularly vulnerable to long-term damage as a result of misuse.

The misuse and abuse of alcohol is a common coping mechanism in major depression, so it is vital that, if we are depressed, we are honest enough to examine and face up to our behavioural patterns in this area. Because we live in a society where taking alcohol at all ages is socially acceptable, it is understandable that alcohol is often the port we turn to during the storms of depression. But alcohol can lead to further drops in mood and, more seriously, to a significantly increased risk of self-harm and suicide.

I recommend that a person suffering from depression abstain from alcohol for a three- to six-month period, or at least until their mood is fully recovered. Many people who suffer from depression, take account of alcohol's mood-lowering effects and abstain. If the person is addicted, alcohol use must cease permanently.

## Learning To Recognise And Treat Stress Triggers In Our Lives

As I detailed in my book *Toxic Stress*, stress plays a major role in triggering depression. Stress is a significant problem in modern life. The pressures of paying for housing, commuting, broken relationships, and the economic downturn, with resulting unemployment, and the rapidly increasing pace of life are all taking their toll.

Reviewing stress factors in our lives often involves being honest with ourselves and those around us. We must not be afraid to make major changes in employment, relationships and financial matters.

Dealing with stress involves examining other lifestyle areas which we have already dealt with: exercise, nutrition, supplements and alcohol intake. Other ways of tackling depression are yoga, meditation, reflexology, and spending time with Mother Nature in parks, forests, beaches, rivers and lakes. Safeguarding mood for the future usually involves recognising how human and frail we all are, trying to be realistic in our assessment of what we should to be doing on a day-to-day basis, and implementing the above lifestyle changes.

## What Is Talk Therapy?

Talk therapy, often called 'psychotherapy', is a means of treating psychological or emotional problems through verbal and non-verbal communication. It involves treating psychological distress by talking with a specially trained therapist and learning new ways to cope rather than using medication alone. Talk therapy is done with the immediate goal of helping the person increase their self-knowledge and awareness of their relationships with others.

Talk therapy assists people in becoming more conscious of their unconscious thoughts, feelings and motives. Its long-term goal is to make it possible to replace destructive patterns of behaviour with healthier, more successful ones.

It has long been recognised (particularly since the 1960s, due to the pioneering work of Albert Ellis and Aaron T. Beck) that talk therapy is a crucial part of the recovery process in major depression. This is because negative thinking, as we have seen, is such a powerful emotional force in the life of the person with this condition. We have to learn new ways of challenging these thoughts; otherwise, we will struggle to get better.

Underlying stress triggers and early negative life experiences may have initiated a bout of depression. Talk therapy helps us deal with these triggers and experiences. The type of talk therapy has actually been shown to be less important than the empathy bond set up between the therapist and the person in difficulty.

There are many different forms of talk therapy, including counselling, psychoanalytic psychotherapy, cognitive behaviour therapy, behaviour therapy, interpersonal therapy, supportive psychotherapy, brief dynamic psychotherapy, and family therapy. There is a place for all of these forms of talk therapy.

## Counselling Therapy

Simply talking about one's depression helps ease emotional pain. Some have experienced abuse, bereavement, addiction and stormy relationships in their past, or have difficulties coping with domestic or work-related stress. The aim of counselling is to help identify problem areas and examine possible solutions. This therapy can be non-directive: the person is encouraged to articulate their problems and work through them with minimum interference from the counsellor.

## Supportive Psychotherapy

Supportive psychotherapy is used in the early stages of treating illnesses like depression. It is widely employed by family doctors and psychiatrists. It involves brief regular meetings with the person in difficulty – at which they are encouraged to deal with short-term life or psychological crises. A classic example might be where somebody is started on an antidepressant but needs support and encouragement until it kicks into action. Supportive psychotherapy is an ideal form of 'talk therapy' in many of the short-term acute crises so often presenting to the family doctor/therapist – such as relationship breakups, work pressures and workplace bullying.

## Interpersonal Therapy

This focuses on the importance of interpersonal relationships in our lives, particularly in relation to depression. It helps the person understand how to deal with conflicts and disputes within the relationship sphere. It may involve problem-solving, dealing with areas like grief, and mechanisms for resolving potential future interpersonal issues.

## Family And Couple Therapy

This form of therapy can be a powerful tool for dealing with depression – particularly in children and teenagers. It focuses on the individual within the social context of the family, and sometimes regards the family as the client. Although this therapeutic process originally involved the inclusion of the entire family, today family therapy can be held in one-to-one sessions, as well as in family, group or couple sessions, led by a trained psychotherapist. In couple or marital therapy, the principles of family therapy are applied to a marital couple, or to those in an equivalent relationships.

## Psychoanalytic Psychotherapy

This is the oldest form of psychotherapy: its origins lie in the pioneering work of Sigmund Freud and his rival Carl Jung. Psychoanalytic psychotherapy focuses on underlying, often unconscious, sources of an individual's emotional or mental problems. It is based on the concept that much of our behaviour, thoughts and attitudes are regulated by the unconscious part of our mind and are thus not subject to ordinary conscious control.

## Cognitive Behaviour Therapy (CBT)

This is a form of talk therapy which is gaining increasing popularity in the treatment of depression.

COGNITIVE refers to mental processes such as thoughts, ideas, perceptions, memories, beliefs, and the ability to focus attention, reason and problem-solve.

BEHAVIOUR refers to 'what we do' and just as importantly 'what we avoid'.

THERAPY refers to a particular approach used to deal with a problem or illness.

CBT is based on two simple but profound concepts:

- Our thoughts influence our emotions, which in turn influence our behaviour. So what we think affects what we feel and do.
- It is not what happens to us in life but how we choose to interpret it!

CBT helps us to challenge the negative emotions, thoughts and behaviour associated with depression and is very much rooted in the present moment.

Understanding CBT is as simple as ABC!

## 'A' Stands For Activating Event

The event that sets up a particular chain of thoughts, emotions and behaviour. It can refer to an external event, either present or future, or an internal one, such as a memory, a mental image, a particular thought, a dream, and so on.

A useful way of examining the activating event is to divide it into:

- The 'trigger', which relates to the actual event which starts the ball rolling.

- The 'inference' we assign to the trigger, or how we view the event which has occurred. In many cases, this involves assigning a 'danger' to the triggering event. 'Why is it bothering us?'

## 'B' Stands For Belief

An all-encompassing term which includes our thoughts; the demands we make on ourselves, the world and others; our attitudes; and the meaning we attach to internal and external events in our lives. It is through these that we 'assess' the trigger and interpretation described in 'A' above. They can be seen as the lens through which we focus on our internal and external worlds. In practice, they often present as demands we make of ourselves – some reasonable, others not!

## 'C' Stands For Consequences

An all-encompassing term which includes emotional and behavioural responses resulting from 'A' and 'B' above.

Let's examine an example of this in action. John, who is due to sit his driving test in two days, becomes very anxious. If we were to do an 'ABC' on his problem, it would look like this:

A: Activating Event
- Trigger: His upcoming test.
- Inference/danger: He might not pass his test.

B: Belief/Demand: His internal 'thought/demand' is 'I must pass my test; if I don't, then I will be a failure.'

C: Consequences
- Emotion: Anxiety
- Physical reactions: John's stomach is in knots, he has tension headache, and sighs constantly to relieve tension.
- Behaviour: He stops eating (as a result of his stomach being upset, due to anxiety), and wonders if he should find an excuse to cancel the test.

We will be examining how the ABC system of CBT can help us in depression later in this book.

Mindfulness-based Cognitive Therapy helps reduce depression relapses by teaching us to become mindfully 'aware' of thoughts, emotions and behaviour in the present moment, so that we can learn to recognise unhelpful patterns, and gradually change them.

The key message here is that talking about our emotions in depression is crucial to getting better!

Of note, there has been a drive particularly in the UK to train family doctors in brief cognitive behavioural interventions to try and assist them in the care of those with mild to moderate depression. It is difficult for GPs however given the severe time pressures they work within however to deliver these interventions.

## Internet-based Cognitive Therapy

There has also been increased interest in providing CBT therapy via the internet especially where therapist driven. This has been very much piloted in the UK with variable results.

The concept was created to overcome one major obstacle relating to the dearth of fully trained CBT therapists available to assist those in difficulty during a bout of depression. it is usually composed of a 6 to 8-week series of sessions with or without a facilitating therapist at hand to assist the process. More success has been achieved with the former.

The general view is that CBT delivered in this manner is more effective to manage patients in general practice than routine supportive therapy.

## What About Drug Therapy?

Another, often controversial, form of treatment for depression involves the use of medication. Some maintain that antidepressants are simply placebos, and work by tricking the mind into believing it is getting better. Others compare their use to that of taking Paracetamol for a headache: it deals with the symptoms but not the causes.

Some believe that antidepressant medications are addictive. Users of antidepressants often complain that the drugs make them feel numb, eliminating some of the symptoms of depression, but also leaving them unable to experience happiness. Another common argument against the drugs is that they have no discernible impact on suicide rates, and that in some cases they may be increasing the risks of a suicidal act. Another concern is that in some cases we are medicalizing sadness or unhappiness which is being created by the life circumstances being experienced by the person who presents with emotional distress.

It is important to acknowledge these concerns. There are elements of truth to many of these accusations. But as with everything in life there is not just a black or white solution to the conundrum of antidepressant therapy.

So what is the truth? Antidepressants are extremely useful as part of a total holistic therapy package for the treatment of major depression. Many find themselves feeling physically exhausted, lacking in concentration, negative and apathetic about themselves, and struggling just to survive; these people often benefit from using antidepressants. As we will be examining later, these drugs can be invaluable in helping the person become functional again. Many CBT therapists and indeed counsellors with experience of dealing with depression quickly realise that it is hard to help a person deal with their negative thinking and emotional difficulties when they are feeling so poorly.

Combining drug therapy with a sensible lifestyle plan can help the sufferer reach a point where they can genuinely embrace talk therapy. A useful way of looking at this is to consider the following: 'Drug therapy helps us to *feel* better so that we can involve ourselves in talk therapy, which helps us to *get* better!'

Research has strengthened the clinical impression among clinicians that major depression is best treated with a combined approach of drug and talk therapy allied to lifestyle changes. Despite this, negative media coverage of drug therapy in particular has created a lot of confusion in the minds of those who seek help for depression. We will be examining individual stories later in the book, but the key message here is that we should never ignore the positive benefits of these drugs, while accepting that they do of course have side effects.

It is not necessary for you to understand exactly how these drugs work: if you are interested, you can find this information in some of my other books. For now, all we have to know is that they 'buzz' the two main mood cables (the serotonin and noradrenaline cables), which lead to a rise in mood and a significant improvement in fatigue, concentration, memory, sleep, appetite and general mental outlook. The most commonly used antidepressants are the SSRIs, which mainly affect the serotonin cable. A second group, called SRNIs, affect both the serotonin and noradrenaline cables. A full description of the names of the main types of these drugs is included in the appendix.

There are some practical observations to make:

- If starting a course of antidepressants, accept that, in order to achieve maximum effect, you should complete the course, which typically runs for six to eight months.
- It is important at the beginning to decide, with your doctor, exactly how long the course will last.
- The SSRIs are the treatment of choice in the majority of cases, but they have side effects, including initial nausea (due to initial activation of serotonin receptors in the gut) and, in some cases, agitation, sweating, tremors of the hands, and heavier periods in the case of females (through their effects on blood platelets). These side effects often disappear after a while as the body adapts to the medication.
- Many people taking SSRIs for depression suffer from a loss of sexual libido, impotence, and delayed or abnormal orgasm. For some, this is not a significant problem, as, due to their depression, they had little or no sex drive anyway. However, after several months of treatment, people will generally start to feel better and will regain their interest in sexual activities. It is then that any sexual side effects caused by these drugs become an issue.
- If side effects occur, they will generally disappear within a few days of finishing the course.
- If we stop these drugs suddenly, we will experience dizziness and a sense of spinning, which is relieved immediately once we start taking the drugs

again. This is why it is important to follow directions from your family doctor to the letter.

- When a course is over, your doctor will explain how to come off the medication.
- They are not addictive, and generally do not cause drowsiness.
- They should generally be taken in the morning, with food.
- The biggest problem is that many are treated with doses that are too small, and the dose is not increased swiftly, as required.
- If the SSRIs are not effective on their own, drugs that affect both the serotonin and noradrenalin mood cables are the next option. Extra side effects, like severe sweating and headaches, can be a problem.
- These drugs will only be effective in up to 70 to 80 percent of cases. Where they are not, a review of the diagnosis is essential, and applying other parts of the holistic pathway, such as lifestyle changes and talk therapies, will usually solve the problem.
- If you are misusing or abusing alcohol, hash or cocaine, and not informing your doctor, you will struggle to get your mood back up, and are only fooling yourself!
- In the elderly, drug therapy should be part of a total package, and should be started in doses half that of the normal.
- There is significant interest in finding antidepressants with a completely clean profile (i.e. with no side effects). There is little doubt that within the next five to seven years, we may have such an option. Until then, it is sensible to use the medications in existence where appropriate; many people have found them to be a useful aid in their journey back to health.

### Why Do So Many Fear Drug Therapy And Is This Fear Justified?

Over many years of walking with patients on the road of MD I have come across a common trend of reluctance to go down this road. The first and usually the most relevant concern is that of stigma and shame – 'what will people say including loved ones or work colleagues if they hear I am on drug therapy for depression'! This belief is strengthened by the negative image the person with MD already have about themselves – 'I am just worthless'!

Other concerns are that they will become hooked on them for life; or that their personality will be somehow altered or that – 'they will simply mess up my head'! Or that they will end up being left on them for long periods; that they will make them drowsy or confused; or that only weak people take anti-depressants. The list can be endless. In my experience, many of these concerns whilst very valid do not actually occur in practice.

At a wider society level, there are deep suspicions of any drug that might be used to treat conditons such as depression. there is good reason for many of these concerns but similar concerns are not expressed for example about many drugs used to treat heart disease or diabetes. Whilst everybody is concerned about the risk profile (with some justification in young age groups) of self harm and suicide – they must also examine the significant risk of an untreated bout of depression in all age groups. There is a concern that these medications may increase suicidal ideation in those under the age of twenty-five, and most countries have a black box warning on the packet to highlight this. This risk is most common in the first few weeks of treatment so this group need to be very carefully monitored for this initial period if placed on these medications.

To debate on the pros and cons of both sides of the drug therapy conundrum is beyond the compass of this book.

As a family doctor who has helped countless patients through individual bouts of MD I have remained quite pragmatic about their usage. They do have side effects and for some these can be significant. But in a significant number of cases, I have found them to be of assistance in an overall package of measures in moderate to severe depression. If, however a patient wants to choose another road then I will walk that road with them as well. It is also my sincere hope that research which is ongoing all the time will eventually produce a cleaner more effective range of drug therapy options that might sort out the present conundrum!

## Can Major Depression Be Treated Without Using Drug Therapy?
The answer to this is unequivocally 'yes'! Some people who suffer from bouts of mild to moderate depression will manage with a sensible mixture of lifestyle

changes and talk therapy. Others may use alternative preparations like St John's Wort. There are issues with the latter; those interested in them should see *Flagging the Therapy*. Moreover, some people are unable to take antidepressants due to side effects of various kinds. Others have major difficulties with taking any type of drugs for depression. It is important to respect the position of these people. For some, family members have had negative experiences with the psychiatric system and drug therapy. Another difficulty is disapproval by family members of drug therapy; this can end up with the person in difficulty rejecting this option.

But there are many who will struggle without drug therapy. These people are often simply not functioning in their everyday lives. They may find it impossible to engage in talk therapy, and unable to concentrate or remember what is being discussed. Many of the cases we will be dealing with later form part of this group; these people are suffering from severe depression. In such cases, drug therapy can be a life-saver.

In these cases, medication can allow the person to regain normality in their day-to-day life. The return of normal mood and an improvement in fatigue, concentration, sleep, appetite, memory and drive allows them to examine the issues that are causing difficulties for them.

# PART TWO

If you are suffering from significant depression as you are reading this section, the chances are that you are feeling miserable. You may be completely exhausted, have difficulty in concentrating on the words you are reading, not be sleeping well, and be unable to enjoy the normal things of life. Allied to this, you may well be feeling very down and may even be having thoughts of self-harm. You may even be actively thinking of ending it all and planning how to do it.

So when I suggest embarking on a journey back to mental health, you may justifiably argue that you are having difficulties just getting up in the morning – never mind starting such an odyssey! You may feel that nothing can help and that, indeed, you are not worth saving.

I ask you to consider a new road whose final destination is a place where deep-seated emotional pain, fatigue and relentless self-criticism and self-loathing is a thing of the past. For those filled with thoughts of self-harm, this is a much easier path to follow than the one they are considering.

The journey I am going to ask you to begin is one that many with major depression have travelled – becoming better as a result. Before undertaking such a journey, there are a number of key questions we need to ask:

- Do we want to undertake the journey at all?
- Do we need a map?
- Can we make the journey on our own, or do we need company?
- Do we need a guide?
- Do we know anyone who has undertaken the journey, so that we can learn

about the route, and any difficulties we may encounter along the way?
- Do we need to break up the route into several sections, with clear stopping points along the way?
- What is our final destination, and what will we do when we get there?

When we are starting a journey from major depression to positive mental health, we need to ask very similar questions:

- Do I have depression at all?
- If I do, do I want to start on a journey back to mental health?
- Do I need a map or manual to assist me on the way?
- Do I need a guide (a doctor or therapist) to accompany me on the journey?
- Do I need the support and knowledge of others who have 'made it'?
- Would it be a good idea to break up the journey back to mental health into a number of achievable sections?
- Do I know what to do when I reach my goal of mental and physical well-being?

If you suffered from a physical illness like diabetes or coronary heart disease, it would be easy to answer the above, and clear that you would undertake such a journey. But depression is a unique illness because it attacks the core of our inner emotional world. It sends this world into a negative spiral which threatens to swamp our logical brain. It is harder to begin a journey when our emotional mind and brain are already dismissing it as being too difficult to undertake.

'There is no point in starting.' 'I am too worthless to be saved.' 'It is too exhausting and pointless for me to even consider starting such a journey.' These negative thoughts pour out of our emotional brain, overpowering thoughts of recovery. This is why many with depression struggle and lead lives of inner despair and deep emotional pain.

Once you understand that it is your emotional brain creating these negative thoughts, it becomes easier to counteract them. We must recognise and understand our enemy in order to defeat him.

A great thought to embrace if you are suffering from depression and fighting such thoughts is: 'Sometimes we can't *think* our way into right action, but we can *act* our way into right thinking!'

So even if your thoughts suggest that there is no chance of reaching good mental health, we can still make a decision to begin the journey and see how things go. Just making such a decision will turn our thoughts into a more positive mode.

I am going to assume that you are prepared to take this journey. I am going to break up our journey into four steps:

- Making the decision that we are suffering from depression, deciding that we want to start the journey back to mental health and choosing a guide to accompany us on the way;
- Examining how to 'feel better', with a modern, holistic package;
- Moving on to learn how to actually 'get better';
- Finally, learning how to 'stay well', once we have achieved the last two objectives (i.e. 2 and 3)!

This journey will take place over a period of between six and twelve months, depending on the person. Like all journeys, it will rarely be without trials and difficulties, but it will also have moments of deep personal insight and joy.

There is an old Irish proverb which states that 'two shorten the road'. What this means is that if we have company on a journey, it is less lonesome: we seem to arrive at our destination without realising it. Nowhere is this more apt than when we are travelling the road out of/away from depression.

This is where Dr Bill will come into his own. We are also going to meet a number of people who are struggling with depression and see how they fared at different stages of their journey back to well-being.

## Dr Bill: Our Expert On Depression

Dr Bill specialises in helping those with major depression and examining how it affects their mental and physical health. He uses a holistic approach to dealing with this illness. In particular, he uses simple CBT concepts to help his patients get well and stay well. He is also a keen proponent of the importance of lifestyle changes.

As we encounter the challenges facing sufferers on this journey, Dr Bill will be dealing with the misconceptions and misunderstandings hampering the management of depression. He will seem to be reading your mind and answering questions you want to ask but don't know who to approach.

Many assume that what is happening to them when they are depressed is unique. In practice, you will see that the same issues come up over and over again. When we are in our emotional shells during depression, we fail to realise that countless thousands are experiencing the same traumas, negative thoughts and exhaustion. For many, this insight is enormously helpful, as it means that we are not alone on the journey.

If you are up to the challenge of such a journey, then let's move on to taking that crucial first step!

# PART THREE

## Step One (Now!)
## Your Journey Begins

If you decide to begin this journey, you have just overcome your first major obstacle. For every journey must begin with a single, often faltering, step! Step One will involve:

- Accepting that our symptoms are due to major depression
- Making the decision to begin the journey to recovery
- Choosing a guide to assist us on the path

### Accepting That Our Symptoms Are Due To Major Depression

Depression plays so many tricks with the emotional brain that we sometimes convince ourselves that we have:

- a physical illness such as diabetes or anaemia
- a stress-related condition
- an anxiety disorder
- a personality 'weakness'

The first three are common conditions that need to be ruled out. This is why we need a guide to assist us. But there are key differences between all four conditions and major depression: physical illnesses like infections, diabetes and anaemia can make us feel unwell, fatigued and out of sorts. But they do not cause the extreme drops in mood, suicide thoughts, major sleep and appetite disruption, difficulties with concentration and drive, and negative thoughts so typical of depression.

Toxic or chronic stress is a great 'mimic' of depression. Many of the typical physical symptoms like fatigue, poor concentration, sleep difficulties and loss of interest in food and sex may be present. We may even feel flat in terms of mood. But it is the severity and depth of the physical and psychological symptoms in depression that helps eliminate stress as the culprit. In depression, for example, we simply don't care what happens – which is not the case in toxic stress.

There is huge confusion between anxiety and depression. Many people assume that anyone with a panic attack must be suffering from depression. The two conditions may occasionally occur in the same person but they are completely distinct. In anxiety, we are worried about what will or won't happen in our lives. In depression, we simply don't care what happens, having neither the interest nor the energy to be concerned.

A common misconception amongst both sufferers and the general public is that depression is a personality weakness. This is one of the great false myths of our time, but so many people with depression come to believe it. Depression is an illness, not a personality problem. It is a condition that affects the mood system in the brain and is both physical and psychological in nature. Our personality is all about who we are as people and how we behave.

Another major issue for many with depression is: 'How do I come to terms with this diagnosis and all that it entails for me personally and those close to me?' And 'What will the social and employment consequences of this diagnosis be?'

Many assume that:

- if they accept the diagnosis, they are doomed to a life of misery
- those close to them will be ashamed to be with them, or even shun them;
- employers will assume that they are 'weaker' than a 'normal person' and should not be put under any stress or pressure at all
- they may be stigmatised at work by employers and co-workers;
- it is an untreatable illness

- they would be better off either denying its presence to themselves and others or even, in some cases, considering self-harm as a way of dealing with the sheer awfulness of such a diagnosis

It is well worth challenging some of the above statements.

The truth is that:

- this is a completely treatable condition
- there is no evidence that a bout of depression means that we will have a life of misery
- although some have a misguided notion that those with depression are somehow weaker, the truth is that many with this illness end up being much stronger emotionally than those who view them as such
- denying its presence is just going to make the problem worse, as we can only deal with it by acknowledging that it is an issue in our lives
- thoughts of self-harm are just a sign of our mood being very low. The reality is that there are a whole host of people who love and care for us and are more than happy to help us on the journey. But we must open up to them
- the negative thoughts pouring out of our emotional brain are the problem, rather than the diagnosis itself. We must challenge these thoughts. Dr Bill will show us how to do that later
- although some employers still live in the dark ages of the nineteenth century and stigmatise employees with depression, there is increasing recognition amongst modern progressive companies that depression is an illness. Many are putting in place support mechanisms to help sufferers recover quickly and facilitate an early return to full employment. They have learned that this approach is actually very cost-effective
- as this century, with its emphasis on 'the mystery of the brain', advances, we will put to bed once and for all misconceptions about this illness

It is important to achieve this first objective of accepting the diagnosis as depression. Some may be relieved by recognising and accepting that this is the condition that is causing them distress. They may be happy to advance to the next step. Others may find accepting this diagnosis more difficult. They may need to attend a family doctor or therapist for reassurance that all other possibilities have been eliminated. This is both sensible and strongly recommended.

The crucial thing is not to withdraw and hide. A useful way of looking at the negative thoughts preventing you from making this jump is to regard them as 'bullies'. If we give in to bullies in everyday life, we empower them; if we challenge them, they retreat.

If you can recognise and accept depression as being a physical as well as a psychological illness, you are truly well on the way to turning the red flag of depression into the green flag of normal mood.

## Making The Decision That We Want To Begin The Journey To Recovery

Once we decide that the likely explanation for the way we are feeling is depression, things get a little easier. The next hurdle is deciding whether you want to do something about it. If one is suffering from high blood pressure or migraine, the answer in general would obviously be 'yes'. But depression is not an ordinary illness, in that, when we are down, our emotional brain attempts to convince us that there is nothing that anybody can do to help us.

Many are so exhausted, apathetic, lacking in interest or drive and filled with self-loathing that they cannot even contemplate starting such a journey. They are just struggling to get through the next few hours and days.

Let's examine a few typical negative thoughts:

- 'There is little that anybody can do to help me.'
- 'Nobody could really understand the way I feel: it's just me and the way I am.'
- 'I have neither the energy nor the interest to even bother looking for assistance.'
- 'Depression is just a weakness anyway: it's up to me to try and snap out of it.'
- 'I shouldn't be bothering other people: I'm just not worth it.'

We could put together a book on the possible negative thoughts in this vein.

But are all these thoughts true? Let's challenge some of the statements above:

When depressed, we feel completely alone and isolated. But the idea that nobody can help us is untrue. There are loved ones and good friends who are often more than happy to help us on the journey. There are also many excellent self-help groups, like Aware, that are there for us when it really matters. There are also a whole host of excellent family doctors and therapists who are trained to be of real help in depression.

We may feel that nobody can understand what is happening to us when we are depressed. In practice, the symptoms and signs of this illness are almost identical the world over, like the symptoms of diabetes and heart disease. Most trained doctors and therapists genuinely understand 'where you are'. There are also many sufferers voluntarily working with self-help groups who are 'expert' in the condition and are more than happy to share their experiences with others.

When depressed, we are genuinely exhausted and struggling. We may feel that we just don't have the energy to seek assistance. But would we feel the same way if we had anaemia or diabetes? In reality, we would usually seek out help in dealing with these illnesses. So even if we are struggling, it is worth making that first step; we will find that these crippling symptoms no longer take over our life!

Depression is not a weakness but a genuine illness: it is our negative emotional brain triggering this thought. In the first part of this book, we have already shown just how 'physical' this illness really is.

The thought that there is little point in bothering other people is extremely common in depression. In reality, there are many people who care and love us and believe that we are of immense worth! They form a treasure trove of support for those who are brave enough to open up to how they are feeling.

## Choosing A Guide To Assist Us On The Path

If we have achieved the first two objectives, our next task is finding a guide to accompany us on the journey. This can sometimes prove to be extremely difficult to achieve. For many with depression, the thought of opening up to anybody about their emotional pain is a step too far.

Research suggests that men find this almost impossible to do. Women will find it difficult but are more hard-wired, emotionally, to seek a guide.

Once again, it is our negative emotional brain which is causing the obstacle, for it generates a host of reasons why we should not seek out such a guide. There are two questions we need to ask:

- Should I seek a guide at all?
- If I do, who should it be?

### Should I Seek A Guide At All?

Why do we need a guide to help us deal with a bout of depression? We can argue that we can do it on our own. But the difficulty with this illness is that many of the thoughts arising in our emotional brain are overwhelming our logical capacity to deal with them. We are experts in our own illness (in that we can explain how we feel) but not in what to do about it. This would be equally the case if we were diabetics.

In both cases, it is better to involve a trained professional, whether a doctor or a therapist. They will assist us on the journey.

Imagine that you were lost in a city. You could wander around for hours, going into many cul de sacs, before, hopefully, eventually arriving at your destination. The smart move would be to seek out a guide who could help you get there more efficiently.

Travelling the road of depression on our own is a lonely, frustrating and mind-numbing experience. If we can find someone who is experienced in helping those with depression to accompany us, we may short-circuit much of this pain and suffering.

### If I Do, Who Should It Be?

There is enormous confusion as to who is the best person to seek out for help with depression. Increasingly, the family doctor is for many the first port of call. They are ideally placed and will often have good empathic relationships with a patient who may be suffering from depression.

Others feel that finding a good therapist or counsellor is the best option. This, in many people's mind, eliminates the risk that they may be prescribed drug treatment for the condition. There are, of course, many excellent therapists who are well trained to assist us on the journey out of depression.

Others assume that we must see a specialist or psychiatrist and to seek out their help on the journey. A final group may seek out a whole host of alternative or complementary therapists.

The crucial step is to seek out a trained professional, either a doctor or therapist, who have both an understanding of this illness and can empathise with you. In many cases, this may turn out to be a combination of both the family doctor (and occasionally a psychiatrist) and a good therapist. Both can play vital roles, either individually or together, in walking with you on the journey. You may start with a therapist who may encourage you to attend your family doctor too. Or you may start with the latter, who may refer you as part of a holistic treatment package to a therapist. The crucial decision is to make the first step and to talk to one of the above.

Let's meet four people suffering from significant depression and examine how they handled the challenges of accepting their illness, deciding to undertake the journey, and choosing their guide.

We will be examining their internal dialogue and giving Dr Bill the opportunity to allay their fears and uncertainties.

## Gerry's Story

Gerry is twenty-two and in real trouble. He started experiencing bouts of depression at the end of his sixth year of school. Initially, he put his symptoms down to the stress of exams. But they followed him into college, where he struggled to cope.

He came from a family where his parents were high achievers and anxious that Gerry would do well at college. He had grown up in an environment where feelings and emotions were never validated, and this led to him being his own biggest critic.

His father was intolerant of conditions like anxiety, stress and, particularly, depression. To him, such individuals were weaklings and very much to be avoided. Gerry unconsciously absorbed these emotional messages and as a result became trapped in his own world of depression. He tried everything to avoid revealing how he felt. In his emotional brain, such an admission would have exposed him to potential ridicule.

He failed his first exam due to exhaustion, poor concentration and difficulties with memory and drive. This was met with stony silence at home and muttered references to laziness and letting the family down. He responded by trying to drown out his feelings of shame and depression with alcohol, which caused his mood to drop further.

He passed his repeat examinations and used all his energies and reserves of stamina to get through his second year of college. But by the middle of his third year, his whole world imploded. His mood fell sharply, his concentration became seriously impaired, and he began to despair. How could he go on? He couldn't study and was clearly going to fail his exams. He struggled to get up each day and isolated himself from fellow students. He lived in a world of emotional pain, exhaustion, constant internal self-flagellation and rumination. He lost all interest in food, and his libido disappeared.

He attended the college doctor, telling him that he was suffering from exhaustion. 'Maybe some tests might explain why' suggested the doctor. When these turned out to be normal, he disguised his feelings of low mood from the doctor. He felt too weak and ashamed to open up about them.

The thought that it would be easier 'not to be here' kept surfacing. He tried to avoid going home, as he didn't know how to explain how he felt. He was also aware of the reception he would receive if he opened up to such feelings of weakness.

He spent more and more time online, trying to make sense of how he felt. He called a depression helpline, which detailed the symptoms of depression, but he blocked out the possibility that he might have depression himself.

Things reached a crisis point on a long bank holiday weekend. His friends had gone home but he couldn't face going home himself. Then, when browsing the web, he came upon a suicide website. They made it seem so easy, and suddenly dark thoughts crystallised in his emotional mind into a definite plan of action.

As he was crossing the college, ruminating on what he would need, he came upon a notice with the number of a helpline for students in difficulty. He decided to give them a ring. The call would both save and change his life.

The girl he talked to was full of warmth and empathy and seemed to sense where he was emotionally. She helped him air his feelings, and persuaded him to attend a college self-help group meeting later that day. She also provided him with numbers for twenty-four-hour helplines if he found himself in further difficulty.

Following this conversation, he felt a slight increase in his mood and decided to attend the meeting. There he met a fellow traveller called Jane. She admitted to bouts of depression and having battled her way through them. She encouraged him to speak to a college counsellor and promised to support him.

Gerry met the counsellor and, with her help, faced the first objective of accepting that his symptoms were most likely due to depression. When he verbalised his thoughts to her, they went as follows:

- 'I now know that these symptoms are most likely due to depression but can't accept the latter diagnosis – so what do I do?'
- 'What would my family and friends think if I did admit to such a diagnosis?'
- 'How could I possibly go home and tell my parents that I have depression?'
- 'Will I end up being thrown off my course if my lecturers learn that I have developed this illness?'
- 'Maybe I am just suffering from stress or am just a weak personality?'

She listened with empathy and helped him examine the validity of these thoughts. He began to accept that his symptoms were not due to stress but to depression. She reassured him that she could interface with the college authorities if necessary to help him defer his course for a year to allow him to deal with the depression which was plaguing him. They also discussed the distinction between mood and personality, and he accepted that his difficulty lay with the former. She then moved him on to his next objective: making the decision to start on a programme of recovery.

Once again, the negative thoughts started flowing through Gerry's mind:

- 'What's the point? There is nothing anyone can really do to help.'

- 'How can I face such a journey? I am finding it a struggle just to get up each day.'
- 'Am I worth saving?'

The college counsellor encouraged him to continue attending her and the depression self-help group. In the group, he ended up having a long conversation with Jane. This turned out to be a watershed moment. She shared with him how severe her own depression had been and how difficult, but ultimately rewarding, her journey had been. She challenged his negative thoughts and shared with him how she faced her own demons. With the help of the counsellor and Jane, he finally accepted not only that he had depression but that he was ready to accept help.

He now had to face the last hurdle: who would be his guide for the journey. This was the moment of truth. Jane was of great assistance and recommended Dr Bill, who had played a key role in her own journey back to health. The counsellor also promised to be with him every step of the way.

With the help of a simple helpline, a supportive peer selfhelp group, a fellow sufferer, and a warm empathy response from a well-trained counsellor, Gerry was now, at last, ready to begin the journey which would transform his life. Later, we will see how he progressed.

KEY MESSAGE
No matter how low, hopeless and despairing we feel, there are so many warm, loving people there for us. If serious thoughts of suicide are flooding into your mind, and you are researching methods to make them a reality, remember that it is the depression that is creating and maintaining these thoughts.

Many will feel that *they* are the problem and that removing themselves will solve the issue. If you can relate to this, then remember: you are a special person loved by many people. It is the condition which is the problem, not you!

Try to avoid websites which lead you down dark roads. Seek out sites and helplines which will give you the information and support you need. At the end of this book is a list of some of the most useful sites and helplines.

## Mary's Story

Mary is twenty-nine and a successful businesswoman. She has been living with her long-term boyfriend for over five years. All her life, she has controlled events. Her life was orderly, if incredibly busy. She had experienced a period of low mood while at school, but no recurrences since.

Then her world disintegrated. Her sister's son took his own life, and his mum went through a very difficult year. Mary spent long periods supporting her. Her job became more stressful as the economic situation imploded. Several of her colleagues were let go, and her workload piled up. She spent longer periods at work trying to catch up. Her relationship began to suffer from the longer absences. She and her boyfriend started to row more. Then her partner's job became more precarious as he was moved to a three-day week. They had taken out a mortgage when the economy was at its peak and suddenly money was becoming a worry. If he lost his job, they would be struggling with repayments.

She became increasingly anxious and stressed. Her partner began to drink more, leading to further rows. Everywhere she looked, someone seemed to want something from her. She started to have difficulties with sleep, and became increasingly fatigued. She struggled to keep up with work projects, and her employer put more pressure on her to get results.

Her partner always wanted to have children, and this became another flashpoint. She felt that they couldn't financially or practically cope with rearing a child at this time.

Her mood began to drop at an alarming rate. She found herself crying all the time, struggling to concentrate, constantly fatigued, and not sleeping. She lost all interest in food and started to lose weight. Her diet consisted of coffee, chocolate, and little else of substance. Her libido dived, and this led her partner to assume that she was either losing interest in him or having an affair. Once again, this led to further rows.

She lost enjoyment in everything, becoming completely apathetic. Her emotional brain turned completely negative and she began to hate herself. She couldn't see any way out of the black hole into which she had descended. She began to resent her partner. How could he not see how she was feeling?

Finally, he had had enough of the rows and silences. This was not the person he had been used to, and he couldn't see any future in continuing the relationship. He just didn't know how to handle Mary in her current state. He mentioned that he was giving serious thought to ending the relationship.

For Mary, this was the last straw. Her mood reached rock bottom, and serious thoughts of self-harm rose to the surface. Before this, she had experienced fleeting thoughts of self-harming, but now they became more concrete. She waited until her partner was away for a day. She then drank an excessive amount of alcohol and overdosed on a mixture of medications, including Paracetamol.

As the day progressed, she became increasingly drowsy, and semi-comatose. Luckily, her partner returned earlier than planned, and found her with the empty bottles of alcohol and medications. He called an ambulance and she was admitted to hospital for over a week.

When she regained consciousness, Mary was initially very upset to have been found. Did they not know how much pain she had been in? It would have been better if she had died. Her partner was extremely upset and guilty that he had not realised how much trouble she was in.

In hospital, Mary was visited by a self-harm liaison nurse. Mary found the nurse extremely empathetic and easy to open up to. The nurse suggested that Mary had been suffering from depression and explained how this could have affected her. She recommended that Mary attend a psychiatrist, but both Mary and her partner rejected this offer. She agreed to attend the liaison nurse for counselling and support after leaving the hospital. At home, she struggled to accept that she could be depressed. Various thoughts flowed through her emotional mind:

- 'I am just stressed, not depressed!'
- 'Maybe I am just a weak personality – and I need to just work harder and overcome these difficulties.'
- 'If I do admit to being depressed, what will my partner do? Will he leave me?'
- 'What will work do if I were even to suggest the possibility that I'm

depressed? Will they see me as a weak link?'

The liaison nurse continued to work with her, and she gradually accepted the diagnosis. She agreed to see Dr Bill, whom the nurse highly recommended – but not before having to counteract the usual negative barrage coming from her emotional mind:

- 'What's the point?'
- 'I just don't have the energy or the interest!'
- 'How will I be able to explain to the doctor how I feel?'

She took some time off work, explained how she felt to her manager at work, and arranged to see Dr Bill. Her partner, briefed by the liaison nurse, developed a better understanding of exactly what depression is. He offered to accompany her for the first few visits.

With the help and support of the liaison nurse and her partner, Mary started the journey back to normal physical and mental health. Like Gerry, she learned that self-harming was not best way to deal with her emotional pain. She was soon to learn simpler ways of dealing with the this pain. Later, we will see how she progressed.

## Jim's Story

Jim has spent a decade living with depression and despair. He came from a family background where his mother and two brothers suffered from significant bouts of major depression.

Jim was extremely bright, advancing quickly through college. Within three years of joining a multinational company, he found himself as head of a division.

But all this was achieved at a high personal cost. Every step of the way, he had battled constant fatigue, difficulties with concentration, sleep, appetite and becoming increasingly isolated in his personal life. He didn't exercise, and avoided any form of socialising, or tasks that would drain his energies. His internal world was a hell of self-loathing, with constant ruminations on the pointlessness of life and his own existence.

But Jim had become an expert at concealing his emotions. The only person who suspected that all was not well was his mother, who was increasingly concerned about his social isolation. She also recognised elements in her son of herself, and came to believe that he might be depressed.

She tried to reach him but he remained elusive. Jim continued to isolate himself and used alcohol at home to self-medicate his mood.

He increasingly thought about ending it all. The only thing preventing this was a concern that it might tip his mother into a similar spiral. But the longer he remained in pain, the stronger the thoughts became:

- 'I can't see any hope for myself.'
- 'Maybe it would be for the best if I was simply not around.'
- 'I just can't go on!'

The thought that he might be suffering from depression had entered his mind but he blocked it out. He had encountered enough of depression in his own family and had never accepted that it was an illness:

- 'Depression is just a sign of a weak personality.'
- 'It's just who I am. I am the problem, not depression!'

His exhaustion, however, reached a stage where he began to struggle at work. He was advised by his employers to see a doctor for a full check-up.

Jim attends his family doctor, has a full check-up, including blood tests, and is told that he is physically healthy. His doctor, aware of the strong family history of depression, gently inquires about his mood.

His concern and warm empathy triggers an extraordinary response. Jim, for the first time in his life, finds himself crying uncontrollably as the dam held in check for a decade bursts. He cries for more than ten minutes and, with the help of his doctor, opens up to the world of pain he is inhabitating.

When depression is mentioned, he initially reacts strongly against the possibility. But his doctor explains in detail what it is and how it affects a person. He persuades him to attend a colleague, Dr Bill, who specialises in this area.

For Jim, it has been a long struggle both to recognise and to accept that depression has been an unwelcome visitor in his life. We will see how he progresses later.

## Kate's Story

Kate had suffered from anxiety from her early teens. She had been physically and sexually abused by her alcoholic father, before he finally abandoned his family. Her mother, terrified of her husband, was unable to protect her two children. Kate was now twenty-five and, despite her past, found herself in a relationship with a similarly abusive partner. She had a three-year-old child and relied on her partner to help rear him.

She blocked out the abusive insulting comments, the occasional physical violence, and her partner's alcohol problem. Her lifestyle was appalling. Her diet was lacking in real nutritional value; she smoked forty cigarettes a day and never exercised.

Her relationship with her mother was poor, as she had never forgiven her for not protecting her from the ravages of her father. This denied her a support base and she became increasingly isolated from family and friends.

Her anxiety levels rose and panic attacks began – which threatened to confine her to the apartment. She found it increasingly difficult to manage her young son and lost interest in keeping the place clean. She started to become fatigued, losing interest in her appearance, and sex with her partner.

Her mood became increasingly depressed and she lost all interest in food. Her day consisted of cups of coffee and cigarette after cigarette. Her partner became angry that she was not looking after 'all his needs'. He began to beat her and she ended up on a number of occasions cowering in the corner, pleading with him to stop. Her life was slowly descending into hell on earth.

Deep down, she believed that she deserved for this to happen. The darkness in her life began to take over, and suicide thoughts increased. Only love for her little son kept a brake on turning them into a reality.

She had reached a point where the idea of the child accompanying her on such a dark road was getting stronger. How could she leave the child behind to face the abusive behaviour of a partner she had grown to hate?

'I would be better off dead and at peace.'

'Both of us would be happier away from this dark, cold place!'

Kate did not realise that she had sunk into the world of depression triggered by the torrent of abuse she had experienced. Rather, she felt that 'she was the problem' – a 'worthless, useless person that the world would be better off without'. She could understand why her partner treated her the way he did.

She found herself drinking more at home, trying to blot out her emotional pain and despair. This led to further fights and altercations with her partner. Finally, he broke her jaw and she ended up in the local A&E. She lied as to how it happened but her case was passed over to a social worker.

The latter persuades Kate to explain just what has been happening in her life – a huge emotional catharsis for her. She identifies that, apart from her social problems, Kate is extremely depressed, with significant suicidal ideation. They agree that it would be better for her child to be taken temporarily into foster care to allow Kate to receive some assistance.

The social worker arranges for Kate to move into a women's shelter. The abusive partner is sorted out by a visit from the police following a complaint by the social worker and a decision by Kate to charge him with assault.

Kate's journey is just beginning, however. She remains very down and can't see any way out of the dark well she is trapped in. At the shelter, she receives a groundswell of support and empathy. She begins to work with a therapist, who also picks up on her depression and explains how it can affect her. She suggests that Kate attend Dr Bill.

Kate's world is about to change for the better. We will follow her journey later.

## Key Points

There are a number of useful points to be taken from these four stories:

- Depression can arrive in our lives for a variety of reasons: stress, abuse, family history, hurt, financial and employment difficulties, and bullying;

- It can start at different ages of our lives, usually triggered by issues like those discussed above;
- For some, the main triggers are in their past, but for many it is events in their everyday lives that lead to the arrival of depression;
- No matter how it is triggered, there is a common set of physical symptoms, like fatigue, difficulties with food, sex, sleep, drive and concentration; and psychological ones, like low mood, anxiety, self-loathing, negative thoughts about ourselves and the world, and, the most serious, suicide thoughts and plans;
- The manner in which people may find themselves seeking help varies from person to person. *How* doesn't really matter!
- Many with depression genuinely do not fully recognise that the way they are feeling, physically and emotionally, is due to an illness. This lack of insight can be there for long periods;
- Many who do identify it may try and block out the possibility and live in a world of painful denial;
- The person who helps us recognise and accept what is going on in our lives in depression may not be a doctor but a friend, a fellow sufferer, a helpline operator, a liaison nurse, a social worker or a trained counsellor or therapist;
- It will often be somebody with whom we feel empathy who will help us break through;
- The key message is that if you see yourself in the signs and symptoms expressed in this section and stories, you have to make the first and most difficult step of opening up to somebody you trust, and then try and find the strength to start the journey back to health with a suitable guide.

# PART FOUR

## Step Two (0 to 2 months)
## How To Feel Better!

We now move on to the second step. This is learning how to apply a modern holistic package to help us feel better!

But what exactly does that mean? As we saw in the last section, most people with depression who want to start on the journey are feeling completely miserable. They are struggling with energy, drive, appetite, sleep, mood and concentration. Many that have never experienced depression struggle to comprehend just how debilitating this illness can be.

Our first task is to help you break out of this spiral of physical and emotional symptoms. The physical symptoms can make getting through every day a real challenge. It can be difficult when feeling like this to handle significant issues which may have triggered the bout. We need to examine how you can feel better before moving on to deal with the rest.

With a holistic package, how long does it take on average to get back to feeling reasonably well? The answer varies, but the majority will get there within six to eight weeks. Others may take up to three months. If you have achieved this step within eight weeks, you are ready to move on to the third step – how to get better – but more of that later!

Feeling better in practice will mean that your mood is up, your energy has improved, you are eating, sleeping and concentrating better, you have more drive and enjoyment, and you can see light at the end of the tunnel. If you are at present in a bad place, all of the above may seem a long way off.

The important message is that all of this is eminently possible, and often within a relatively short period. It is always best to deal with this step with the help of a trained professional. I would strongly recommend that in general, the best person to do this is your family doctor. If you have a good empathy bond with him or her, it will speed up the whole process. You may also be working with a counsellor or therapist, and that is absolutely fine. But their role at this early stage may be more supportive rather than assisting you deal with deeper issues – this may come later.

You will also notice how resistant you are to applying many parts of the holistic package we will outline. The emotional brain, as we will discover, has an endless supply of reasons why we should ignore much of the advice that is suggested. Typical thoughts might be:

- 'It's just too difficult!'
- 'I can't find the energy or enthusiasm to do it.' 'Nothing will make any difference.'
- 'I am never going to get better, so why try?'
- 'I am worthless anyway, so there is really no point.'

We must start as we mean to continue, and recognise that these thoughts are coming from our emotional brain (which in depression has gone into complete negative mode). So they are just thoughts and not reality! Recognising this can greatly speed up your acceptance of what is necessary in order to start feeling better.

Let's examine how the modern holistic package discussed in the first part of the book can be applied to help us feel better. We will examine it under four headings:

- Empathy
- Lifestyle changes
- The role of drug therapy
- The role of talk therapy.

## Empathy

Your first task on the road to feeling better is to find a doctor or therapist you feel comfortable with, and to engage with them. In Step One, you chose a guide for the journey. But there is a huge difference between choosing a guide, and physically attending them, and opening up as to how you feel.

Part of this difficulty relates to uncertainty as to how to initially open up the subject, and how it will be received! Many attend their family doctor but leave without revealing their distress. They may mention fatigue but disguise their low mood and negative thoughts.

You will know whether the guide you have chosen is the right person if you sense warmth and empathy as you reveal your story. Never be afraid to say at the beginning that you are feeling down, stressed, tired, anxious, or whatever term you feel comfortable using to describe how you feel.

Always explain how you feel *physically* as well as emotionally. If you have a good empathy experience with your guide/doctor/therapist, you have taken a major step in your journey to feeling better.

As discussed earlier, your emotional brain/mind, which drives depression, has been overwhelming your logical brain/mind. This explains the host of negative thoughts running around in your mind. But if you air them in the safe, secure environment of an empathetic relationship, they lose a lot of their negative power.

You will feel an immediate lift in mood after opening up in this way. In the beginning, this, on its own, will only last for a short period. But when combined with other measures that we will be suggesting, it has a strong positive effect.

If you have a negative empathy experience, you may experience the opposite, and your mood may drop temporarily. That should not stop you seeking out a different guide. You have to find somebody to whom you can relate with empathy – otherwise your journey may be more difficult. If your family doctor is helpful but you do not sense this empathy, you may combine working with a therapist as well as visiting your doctor (particularly if you sense an empathy bond with the therapist).

## Lifestyle Changes

These form the backbone of feeling and getting better from depression, and also in its prevention. We dealt with them in general in the first part of the book, but let's examine them in practice.

### Exercise

This is the simplest lifestyle change to make, and one that many find the most difficult to put into practice. When we are very down, we are so tired and apathetic that it is difficult to become involved in any form of exercise.

The fatigue you are feeling when depressed is different from the normal, healthy tiredness one experiences after any physical task. It is a gnawing tiredness which never seems to leave you. It is in fact a form of mental fatigue originating in your emotional brain rather than a physical phenomenon.

Our emotional brain will come up with numerous excuses as to why exercise is not possible. Let's examine a few common thoughts:

- 'If you only knew just how exhausted I am, you wouldn't ask me to do what feels impossible!'
- 'I only have so much energy to expend, and I need to save it for surviving the simple tasks of each day.'
- 'What's the point of even trying? It's a complete waste of time!'
- 'How could simply exercising make the slightest difference? I don't think you know how awful I feel.'
- 'I arrive home and no matter how much I try, I can't make that first step towards going for a walk. I almost feel paralysed!'

Over the years of helping many people with depression, I have heard every possible reason expressed as to why exercise is avoided. The reason for this is that when we are down, we struggle to find the motivation or energy to exercise.

We reviewed earlier the types of exercise we might try, and for how long. Here are some simple techniques to get you started:

- If avoiding any form of exercise, begin with a short period of five to ten minutes for the first few days and gradually increase it up to the ideal of thirty minutes.
- It is often a good idea to write down how low you felt before you started out on your walk and then, when you finish exercising, write down how you felt after it.
- It is an excellent idea to involve a family member or good friend in the process. Ask them to come around at a set time to drag you out for a walk or jog. The advantage of this is that it sets up a routine. You also have the sociability of somebody with you for the exercise period. This is helpful for your mood.
- Try and find an exercise that appeals to you. For many, this may be walking or jogging, but others prefer the gym or the pool. The type of exercise doesn't matter, it is the consistent daily thirty minutes that matters.
- The simplest exercise is a thirty-minute daily walk in the fresh air. It has the advantage of getting you out in the light, which also helps to lift mood.
- Leave your walking shoes close to the front door and try to make yourself go out for a walk before you settle down after a day of working or studying.

If you are sitting at home and can't get moving, here is a light-hearted CBT behavioural technique. Assume you are sitting down and struggling to move. Stand up and put out your right foot and follow it up with your left foot. You have moved a few yards. Now put out your right foot again and follow it up with your left, and so on. Soon you will find yourself at the front door. Now open it. You are in the open, so start walking!

Sometimes when in a bad place, it is impossible to 'talk' our way into action, such as exercise – but we can 'act' our way into right thinking. In practice, this means that we have to make that first move, no matter how much we have convinced ourselves mentally that it is not possible. The benefits of such an action cannot be underestimated in terms of its importance.

Exercise might be the single most important part of your journey back to mental health!

*Nutrition*

Just like exercise, diet plays an important role in helping you feel better. Most people with depression have been eating poorly for some time before seeking assistance. Yet our body, and particularly our brain, desperately needs a steady stream of nutrients in order to function normally. We have detailed earlier the types of foods necessary, and recommended B vitamins and Omega 3 fish oils.

But why do people with depression struggle to eat properly? The answer is that this illness simply kills your whole interest in food: you receive no enjoyment from it. This creates a vicious circle. The less nutrition to your brain, the worse you feel. The worse you feel, the less likely you are to eat, and so on.

So how can we break this cycle? Well, the following points may help:

- It is a good idea to involve family or friends in encouraging you to prepare and eat healthier meals. This also encourages positive socialising.
- I encourage those with depression to regard food as a form of medication. You don't have to 'enjoy' the food itself – just regard it as a necessary part of feeling better.
- Try and eat small, regular meals throughout the day rather than relying on one large meal.
- Try and pick out foods which are helpful to our mood system, as outlined earlier.
- As with exercise, even if you can't find any reason to eat properly, just do it. The positive benefits will make the effort worthwhile.

*Alcohol/Substances*

It is widely accepted that many of those who are feeling very low misuse or abuse alcohol to lift their mood. But alcohol is a drug in itself. It initially will help us relax, and we may even experience a brief improvement in mood for a few hours. But the following day our mood will usually drop further. In some cases, it can increase thoughts of self-harm and even trigger suicide attempts.

I have always felt that a key part of 'feeling better' in relation to depression is taking alcohol out of the equation completely until mood has been restored to normal. I strongly advise that if you want to achieve your goal of feeling better, avoid alcohol completely for a period of two to three months.

You may protest that this is the only lift in mood you get and that it helps you numb the pain. But it is a false friend. To really get rid of your pain, we need to take alcohol out of the picture and concentrate on other key lifestyle changes like exercise and nutrition. The benefits of this will accrue quite quickly.

So also with illegal substances of any type: they have to be removed from the picture. If you are taking hash on a regular basis, it will be difficult to get your mood back to normal. If you are misusing more serious drugs like cocaine, speed or heroin, it goes without saying that it will be impossible to 'feel better' if you do not stop.

Remember, it can take up to six or eight weeks, or longer, for these substances to leave your system. At the end of that period, your mood may come up, even in the absence of other therapies.

### Stress Triggers

When feeling very down, it is not wise at this stage to examine in detail life stressors which are causing you difficulty or stress. But we cannot ignore immediate 'major' stress issues that might prevent us from feeling better.

Some simple examples of this:

- We might be struggling with work due to extreme fatigue, difficulties with concentration and memory, and very low mood. In such situations, work is an acute stress trigger, further bringing down our mood. It will be difficult in such situations to start feeling better. So we may have to take the pragmatic decision, together with our employer, to take sick leave to access the help we need.
- If you are a student at college, once again you may be feeling so miserable that you are unable to attend and focus on key lectures. The stress of this (and of sitting exams you have no chance of passing due to inability to study) is a powerful trigger to bring down mood further. Deciding,

together with the college in question, to take a period out of study for either part of, or all of, a year may turn out to be a very wise move in the long run.

- If you are in a work situation where the primary stress trigger bringing down your mood is systematic bullying, then once again it is not wise to stay in this situation in the short run. Taking time out on sick leave to deal with your own depression, with a plan to try and engage later with your employer in relation to bullying issues, is a better solution.
- If you are a mum who is struggling due to the stress of rearing a new baby and postnatal depression, you are not in a position to simply ignore the stress relating to the former. It is wiser in such situations to seek out help, in the form of family or friends, in order to reduce the burden.
- If you are in serious financial or mortgage difficulties, the stress involved may trigger major depression. In such situations, you may have to face the acute situation and seek out financial or mortgage advice as to how you should proceed.

The secret is to analyse whether the stress relates to an acute problem or to something you could work out later, when you are feeling better. In the case of the latter, it is better to leave dealing with such issues until we move on to the next step. If it is directly impinging on our mood, we have to deal with it immediately. Never be afraid of looking for assistance in such situations. Most families, friends and indeed employers/businesses are willing to help if we open up to them about how we feel.

### Alternative/Complementary Therapies

Many who are feeling down explore the world of alternative therapy because they feel less threatened. I have explored these therapies in *Flagging the Therapy*: if you are interested, you can read about them there.

Most of these therapies are of limited value for the treatment of genuine depression. The only ones that have been shown to be of some help are yoga, mindfulness (for the prevention, not treatment, of depression) and St John's Wort.

If you are using any one of the alternative therapies available, you are probably benefiting from a short-term placebo-type lift in mood, assisted by the empathy relationship with the therapist in question.

If you find this helpful, then by all means continue. But mention to your doctor if you are taking any herbal remedies, as they may interact with other medications.

Recovering from depression requires a more holistic approach. This will involve a fundamental examination of every part of our lives.

## Light Therapies

I feel that these have a genuinely scientific basis. We know that as we sleep, our brain melatonin levels are higher and our serotonin levels fall; and that the reverse is true in the daytime.

In the winter months, our serotonin levels fall. This is because of the lack of sunlight during this period. Daylight encourages serotonin activity, whereas darkness encourages melatonin activity. As a result, many with depression find their mood dropping significantly in the months from October or November till the spring.

So as part of our drive to help us feel better, I encourage you to purchase a dawn simulator for use in these winter months. If you set it to come on an hour before you rise, it will gradually simulate summer light for that period, increasing your serotonin activity and early-morning mood.

Some will go further and have thirty minutes to an hour of light-box therapy on a daily basis. If you are doing this, make sure that the box has at least ten thousand lux in strength. There are details at the end of the book of places where you can purchase light-boxes.

## The Role Of Drug Therapy

In the first section of the book, we examined various forms of drug therapy and the pluses and minuses of their use. Here I examine why you should at least consider their use as part of a package to help you feel better. I am going to answer some common questions asked by patients. We will also examine typical negative thoughts plaguing those with depression in relation to drug therapy.

## Why Should I Consider Drug Therapy At All?

This is a sensible question and one that everybody with depression should ask. The answer is that there are many occasions where we are feeling so low, so exhausted and so lacking in drive, are struggling so much with concentration, sleep and appetite, and are so lacking in enjoyment of anything in our lives that lifestyle changes on their own will not be enough.

'But what about talk therapy?' is the usual follow-on question. Again, this is a good suggestion. There is little doubt that empathy and opening up to how we feel is crucial.

But many are so tired, down and lacking in concentration that they struggle to engage with or even remember the talk therapy in question. I have encountered this on numerous occasions throughout the years.

This is because depression really does 'depress' our normal brain functioning, making it much harder for us to get the best out of talk therapy. As leading CBT therapist Enda Murphy puts it: 'Drug therapy helps us to conceptualise our emotional difficulties.'

Another practical reason for the use of drug therapy as part of our drive to assist us to feel better is that we are all busy people. Whether employers or employees, students, mothers or fathers, we all have key roles to play in society. We need to become functional as soon as possible. And 'functional' is the key word here. To get through our everyday lives, we need energy, drive and motivation.

The greatest strength of drug therapy is its ability to restore these critical functions within a reasonably short period of time. This gives us the opportunity to examine the issues which led us into difficulty to start with. The evidence shows that if you combine drug therapy with lifestyle changes and empathy, the person with depression can feel and function normally within four to eight weeks on average.

It is important to realise from the outset that you can make it without drug therapy. But it may make the journey harder, longer and more frustrating for yourself and those around you! I have always been completely realistic about drug therapy.

Medication does not solve life's problems. Drugs have side effects, as already documented. They are neither the only way to treat depression nor the big bad ogre, as some sections of the media suggest. They are simply a very useful tool to help us both feel better and function normally.

## When Should I Consider Drug Therapy?

A good rule of thumb is to ask yourself: 'Am I functioning normally?' If you answer this honestly, it is easier to decide on drug therapy. If you are only suffering from mild depression, depression with a small 'd', or toxic stress, then the chances are that you will be functioning reasonably normally if you are feeling down. If you are, however, suffering from more significant problems, and finding each day an endless battle just to survive, then consider talking to your doctor about going on a course of medication.

In general, there is little point in waiting longer than four weeks if you are feeling really miserable. It is unlikely that the bout of depression will disappear without help. If you have been making the lifestyle changes suggested and have opened up to somebody about how you are feeling, but are still feeling miserable, then the next step is to consider drug therapy.

## How Should I Take Them?

In general, most antidepressants are taken in the morning, and usually with food. It is often a good idea to take a simple anti-nausea tablet for ten days when starting most of the modern SSRI tablets. This is because it takes the digestive system about that length of time to adjust to them. It is also important to take them at the same time every day. If you miss out on them for more than twelve hours, you may experience a bout of dizziness or spinning. If this happens, just take the medication again, and the dizziness will disappear. This, by the way, does *not* mean they are addictive – just that our brain chemistry has to adjust to their presence.

A few antidepressants may be taken at night, but this will usually be to counteract any drowsiness symptoms.

## How Long Will The Course Be? Will It Be For Life?

This is the big fear of most people with depression: 'If I am put on antidepressants,

I will be left on them for life. Even worse, I will be hopelessly and permanently addicted to them for good!'

The good news is that the majority of people who require drug therapy for depression will only need to remain on it for an average of six to nine months. A good rule of thumb is that most will need to stay on them for six months 'from the time they are feeling better' (which usually takes four to eight weeks). Only in a small number of cases where a person has severe, relapsing depression does the prospect of long-term therapy come into play. Thankfully, this is not the norm.

As for the concept that they are 'hopelessly addictive', the reality is that classical modern SSRI-type antidepressants are not addictive: they do not create the craving which lies at the heart of all addiction. I have yet to see somebody craving an antidepressant!

This confusion arises because many fail to distinguish normal antidepressants from addictive substances like tranquillisers. There is also a lack of understanding about the difference between antidepressants, anti-psychotic drugs (used to treat psychosis), and mood stabilisers (used to treat Bipolar Disorder). Later on, we will be examining what happens when coming off drug therapy – another area which causes confusion.

### What About Side Effects?

Once again, we dealt with most of these in the first section. We have to point out that depression itself is a most debilitating physical and psychological illness. We are already suffering from difficulties with fatigue and usually have no libido. Some patients smile when informed about possible sexual side effects. Statements like 'If you have any idea of just how awful I feel. . . . Sex is just about last on my priority list at this moment in time' are quite telling!

The most common symptoms are nausea, for the first few weeks; some initial agitation, which usually settles within the first ten days; occasional, if minimal, drowsiness, and a reduction in either sexual drive or function. All of these are extremely variable from patient to patient. In my experience, most patients are more than happy to swap them for the world of pain and exhaustion they are presently occupying. It is also important to note that these symptoms will disappear within days of stopping medication.

## But What Will People Say?

For most people with depression, this is the issue which really bothers them. Depression encourages us to think the very worst of ourselves, and to assume that others will think the same. So we live in a world of constant negative self-rating.

In some senses, beginning a course of drug therapy is almost fulfilment of all the negative feelings we have about ourselves:

- 'I always knew I was a weakling; this only confirms it.'
- 'I am so bad that I even have to take tablets. It's the worst thing I could have imagined.'
- 'What would my family and friends think if they heard that I was on antidepressants?'
- 'What would my employers or workmates think of me if they heard I was taking antidepressants?'
- 'They will think I am weak and start to treat me differently!'
- 'Does this mean I am "mad"? Others will certainly think so?'
- 'Will they think of me as being a junkie? After all, aren't these drugs meant to be addictive.'

This is why many struggle to seek assistance for depression. They assume that they will be put on medication, judge themselves as being inferior as a result, and will be judged by others as being so!

### *Let's Challenge Some of These Common Negative Thoughts*

How could taking a course of antidepressants make me a weakling? If we followed that logic, then anyone taking treatment for high blood pressure, heart disease or diabetes, for example, must also be put in the same bracket. But others might say that these drugs act on the 'brain', so they must in some way be altering it. Based on this logic, we have to assume that anyone on treatment for Parkinson's disease or multiple sclerosis must also be in some ways 'altered' – because technically such drugs also act on the brain.

The truth, of course, is that any therapy, including talk therapy in all its forms, ends up 'changing' the brain – but in a positive manner. Similarly, when you exercise, you are actively changing your brain.

Many people, due to a barrage of negative publicity in relation to the use of drug therapy, imagine that using these medications must mean they are really ill. They have no idea what it is about antidepressants that is so evil, but in their minds they have built up an image that the medications are truly awful.

The reality, of course, is that taking tablets for any condition is an issue! But we routinely take treatments for all kinds of conditions and never question their use or truly examine their potential side effects. Classical examples of this include simple analgesics like Ibuprofen and Paracetamol. The number of difficulties, and indeed deaths, associated with both, leave drug therapy for depression in the shade. But we don't regard ourselves as being bad, evil or weak if we use these. We need to regard drug therapy for depression as simply a useful therapy with both positive and negative aspects, similar to other medications used in our everyday lives.

Many become anxious that family and friends will treat them differently on learning that they have started a course of antidepressants. This has its origin in the bad old days of psychiatry, when anybody on drug treatment for any form of mental health issue was considered mad! I often recall my grandmother lowering her voice when discussing 'consumption', as TB was known at the time. Anyone who developed it was much to be pitied and should be spoken of in hushed tones! The problem is stigma – where we associate an illness that we don't really understand with weakness. Thankfully, depression is gradually, like TB, coming out of the dark ages as our understanding of the condition modernises.

If people close to us, such as family and friends, really love us, as they do, they will be supportive and open to us involving ourselves in any form of therapy that will help us feel, and get, better. If they have a problem with this, the difficulty does not lie with us. Rather it is usually due to a lack of understanding, on the part of those close to us, of just what depression is and how it should be managed. Referring them to groups like Aware will often help relieve them of any such misunderstandings.

The whole issue of the way in which depression is handled in the workplace is a much wider one than whether we are or are not on antidepressants. There is a widespread belief amongst many who suffer from depression that informing employers is a death knell for their career! There is also a belief that work colleagues will once again rate us as being weak and much to be pitied.

There is, however, a definite change in the understanding of many employers, with the realisation that this is an illness which, if quickly and properly treated, will help reduce the amount of sick leave the person will take.

There is still a huge job of work to be done to fully revolutionise the understanding of both employers and employees about depression. But the workplace stigma of depression, like that previously associated with TB, will eventually become a thing of the past, as we grow and develop our knowledge of this illness.

Whether we inform employers or not about our depression is a personal decision. It should not interfere with our decision to use, or not use, drug therapy. That decision should be made by you, in consultation with your doctor.

The fear that one will be treated differently if on antidepressants is another common one. It goes back to the concept that they will somehow change your personality and that you will become a different person. This of course relates back to the idea that they will change your brain.

The truth is that our personality is fundamentally different from our mood. All that these drugs are doing is helping to lift our mood; they have no effect on our basic personality, which has been shaped by our genes and upbringing.

Once again, the problem relates to a lack of understanding of just what depression is and how these drugs work. We have already examined the idea that they change the brain: all therapies do the same!

Often providing those close to us with information (such as books like this, or websites like that of Aware) can go a long way to preventing them from treating us any differently than if we were on treatment for, say, high blood pressure.

The other big fear is that if we are on antidepressants, we must be mad.

This is a common anxiety, and we have explained its origins. If you are suffering from depression, you are probably much saner than the author of this book! The real difficulty is that depression is often perceived in the same way as psychosis and schizophrenia, where the person may suffer from altered or disturbed reality. So if I am on medication, I must suffer from one of these illnesses, and thus be seen as mad. (Again, this relates to the bad old days of psychiatry, where such conditions were badly understood and badly treated.)

The reality is that whether or not you take drug therapy for depression, you are completely sane: you are just suffering from an illness that affects your mood. As already outlined, the fastest way to lift your mood in such a situation is to take a course of antidepressants. But the choice, as always, lies with you.

Lastly, one of the most common negative thoughts in relation to drug therapy is that if we use them, we will be considered to be a 'junkie' and doomed to a life of addiction.

This is once again due to the misinformed opinion that all antidepressants are addictive and that we will spend our life craving them. In practice, we now know that simple antidepressants are non-addictive. As before, the provision of sensible information on this issue will reassure those close to us.

## What Do I Do If My Mood Is Not Coming Up After Four To Six Weeks On Drug Therapy?

This is an important question. In general, if your doctor has put you on a course of antidepressants, you will start to feel a good bit better after two to four weeks. If this is not happening by then, it is important to increase the dose of the drug to its maximum. If your mood is still not improving, it is important to move quickly to change to a new antidepressant – with the help of your doctor. In my opinion, too many patients end up remaining either on a dose that is too low or on a drug which is not helping.

In general, with the appropriate antidepressant, if you have a good empathy bond and are making the appropriate lifestyle changes, your mood will come up. If within eight to ten weeks you are still in difficulty, you may need to see a specialist or psychiatrist, as your diagnosis and treatment may need to be reviewed.

In summary, if you are not functioning normally, due to the ravages of depression, then consider drug therapy as part of a holistic package to try and get you feeling better by our goal of four to eight weeks.

## The Role Of Talk Therapy

For those who have not experienced genuine depression, talk therapy would seem like the most natural path to take. But as with many things in life, it is not quite so simple.

For depression, as already outlined, leads to a world where the person is exhausted, struggling with concentration and motivation, and having difficulties with memory, drive and sleep. So at this early stage in the treatment of a bout of major depression, the role of talk therapy may have to take more of a supportive role.

The key, as always, is the severity of a particular bout of depression and how functional the sufferer is. If the bout is mild and the person is able, and willing, to involve themselves in talk therapy (whatever the form), then this is clearly the best road to travel.

If, as is often the case, the person is struggling with significant symptoms of depression, then they will find it difficult to involve themselves in, concentrate on and actually remember the issues that will come up in talk therapy. In such situations, counselling and other significant therapies, like CBT, are a lot less effective at this stage in the treatment path.

At this phase of the journey, talk therapy has two significant roles to play:

- Assisting the person in recognising their condition and encouraging them to seek professional help if this is felt necessary.
- To act as a key support for the person over the first six to eight weeks, when lifestyle and drug therapy combine to help the person feel better.

We will assume that by now you are attending somebody with whom you feel empathy, whether it is your family doctor or a counsellor or therapist. They will assist and support you until you feel well enough to tackle key issues in your past and present life which may be affecting you.

Remember, as discussed before, there are two experts involved in this process. You are the expert in how it feels to be depressed, and they are expert in helping you recognise and deal with it. Together you are a powerful team!

Later, in the next step, talk therapy will become a much more important part of our therapy regimen. Let's now examine how five more people with depression learned how to deal with the second step in the journey back to full health, namely how to feel better!

## Siobhan's Story

Siobhan is twenty-eight and five months postnatal. She had always been a worrier and suffered anxiety in her teens and twenties. She was the classical perfectionist who liked everything in order, particularly in relation to her house and job (as a high-powered secretary to a business executive).

She had married her partner, after they had lived together for five years: the wedding was planned to the last degree. She had no prior history of depression but her mum had suffered a few episodes, starting after the birth of her second child.

Siobhan had found the pregnancy difficult: she had suffered from significant morning sickness and fatigue. However, she never let her standards drop in relation to her work and home, even though she was finding it difficult to do this.

She had watched all her friends seemingly glide through their pregnancies and postnatal period. For her, the arrival of her new baby turned her life upside down. She tried breast-feeding for four weeks but became increasingly anxious and exhausted by the process as her little daughter lost weight. The constant feeding on demand, where she struggled to produce enough milk for the baby, destroyed the secure, ordered world she was used to inhabiting. At four weeks, on visiting the practice nurse to have the baby weighed, she was advised to bottle-feed the baby. She burst out crying and became quite upset. She felt such a failure that she was unable to breast-feed her baby. The nurse reassured her that this was a regular occurrence and that the main concern was to get the baby's weight back to normal.

Although the change to bottle-feeding was a great success and her baby daughter started to put on weight, Siobhan couldn't shake off the feeling that she had failed her. She felt that she was a hopeless mother as she struggled to cope with the arrival of this little bundle in her life.

Her husband was doing his best to assist but she pushed him away: she felt that he did not understand how she felt. This led to rows as he felt rejected. Things began to spiral out of control.

Siobhan became increasingly fatigued and lost interest in food and sex. Her weight fell and she struggled to concentrate on the simplest of issues. Her mood fell dramatically and she started to feel a complete failure as a mother, and indeed as a person.

She fell behind with her housework, as she couldn't be bothered. She found herself unmercifully judging herself in relation to her friends, feeling that she could never match up to them. Her appearance began to suffer as she stopped caring about how she looked.

Her baby became more withdrawn as she struggled to bond with her. At times, she had fleeting thoughts of self-harm, making her feel even more distressed and guilty: 'How could I even contemplate such an action? I have a lovely child and a husband who does, in his own way, care for me. I feel so guilty!'

Piece by piece, the lovely, organised world that Siobhan had built up around her was falling apart. After three months, she was now well and truly exhausted, and feeling trapped in a dark hole from which nobody could help her escape.

For Siobhan, the first step on her road to recovery came when her older sister, Deirdre, came from Australia to visit her. Deirdre was distressed to find Siobhan so down and the house in such turmoil.

Deirdre had had a similar experience after the birth of her second son, and recognised immediately the symptoms and signs of postnatal depression. She had kept this to herself while she was in Australia, not wanting to upset her family back home. She had, however, sought and received help for her depression and had completely recovered.

The revelation that Deirdre, whom Siobhan had always looked up to and regarded as the 'strong person' in the family, had suffered from postnatal depression, came as a complete shock to Siobhan.

The empathy bond with her sister had always been strong, and it helped Siobhan to open up to just how awful she felt, physically and emotionally. The fact that Deirdre had actually taken an overdose before coming to the attention of her doctor also shocked Siobhan.

Deirdre detailed how she had travelled on the road to recovery, and offered to accompany her to see Dr Bill, their original family doctor. He turned out to be very empathetic and understanding of her condition, and went through treatment options for her. He explained that it was common for women to experience a bout of depression in the postnatal period due to a combination of hormonal changes, the massive stress of feeding and looking after a newborn baby, and in some cases having a family history of depression. He gave her some information on the condition to read when she got back home.

He explained that his first job was to help her feel better, and that some lifestyle changes, and perhaps some drug therapy, if required, would greatly help. Later, he would do some work with her on the next step: how to get better.

She was anxious to avoid drug therapy if at all possible but did agree to key lifestyle changes, including exercise on a daily basis, improving her nutrition, taking Omega 3 fish oils, and B complex supplements and avoiding alcohol.

She had some reservations, though:

- 'If the doctor knew how exhausted I feel, he wouldn't ask me to exercise for a full half an hour per day! I can barely get out of bed in the morning, and struggle just to look after my baby, never mind myself.'
- 'Food just tastes like sawdust! I have no appetite and no interest in anything but coffee and chocolate!'
- 'How could simple vitamins and fish oils make any difference to how I feel?'

When she made her feelings known to Dr Bill, he explained that everybody who was feeling down struggled to make these lifestyle changes. He made the following suggestions:

- That she try and start exercising for short periods, perhaps starting with ten minutes, and gradually increase it up to thirty minutes when feeling better;
- That bringing the baby with her, either in a sling or a buggy will encourage her to go out;
- To try and enlist the help of family member or a good friend to accompany her on the walk, as she would benefit from the social dimension, as well as the exercise;
- That she keep a record of how she felt before and after exercising, as this would strengthen the link between the exercise and a rise in mood;
- That walking in the daylight would also help her, as sunlight improves mood;
- That she could also enlist the help of a family member or friend in relation to preparing and eating good meals and ensuring that she take the supplements he had recommended.

While these lifestyle changes helped, her mood continued to fall over the next four weeks, particularly when her sister returned to Australia. She went to visit Dr Bill again.

He felt that her physical symptoms and mood were significantly impaired and suggested a course of antidepressants to try and help her feel better. Although unhappy about doing this, she agreed. After initial nausea (which was helped by a course of simple Motilium), she found that after two to four weeks, her mood began to improve and a lot of her fatigue, and her difficulties with concentration, waned. She found herself thinking more clearly and being better able to focus on her baby daughter, who sensed the change and became more responsive. In the beginning, she struggled with the simple thirty minutes of exercise recommended, but found that popping the baby into a sling encouraged her to make the effort to go out for a walk. She loved the feeling of her snuggled up close and found her mood always better after returning from such a walk.

She also found it difficult to make herself eat properly, but after a month on drug therapy her appetite improved. She was still not getting enough sleep but this was due to her daughter not sleeping. Her husband and mother, now fully aware of what was going on, moved into the breach to assist her by every means possible. Her mother also shared her experiences with Siobhan, who was now starting to feel much better.

By the end of the second month, Siobhan's world was coming back to normal. She was eating and sleeping better, and bonding with both her baby and her husband; her fatigue and concentration were rapidly improving. Her weight recovered. Finally, she was 'feeling better', or as her husband and friends would exclaim, she was 'back to herself!'

Now the real work would begin, as she moved on to the next step, where Dr Bill will assist her in her objective of getting better.

## Dr Bill's Comments

There is much to learn from Siobhan's story:

- Many women struggle in the postnatal period, primarily due to the massive expenditure of energy required to recover from the labour and then look after a small baby in the first three to six months of life.
- The majority recover from this stress, even if they find it an exhausting process. However, a significant number (particularly if they have a history of family depression, significant antenatal anxiety or depression, or experience a very traumatic labour or postnatal period) will develop postnatal depression.
- The symptoms and signs are typical of routine depression, with the added difficulty of bonding with the new baby. The latter makes the sufferer feel even worse.
- The biggest difficulty, as always with depression, is that many women feel that 'they' are the problem and do not come for assistance. Many genuinely do not recognise the symptoms as being due to depression. They just assume that they are 'not coping'.
- In some cases of postnatal depression, a combination of support, information and lifestyle changes will on their own be enough to help the person

feel better. However, in some cases this will not be sufficient; in such situations, drug therapy can be invaluable in helping the person reach a point where they are able to feel better.

Later, we will be examining the thought processes which underlie many cases of postnatal depression.

The good news is that so many with postnatal depression can, with the above holistic approach, swiftly be helped to feel better – with both mother and baby benefiting.

## Paul's Story

Paul is twenty-seven and has suffered from depression since the age of seventeen. He has experienced frequent bouts of extremely low mood, total exhaustion, and poor concentration, along with concomitant sleep, drive, sex and memory difficulties. Suicide thoughts have been a constant companion along the way. His world was at times a dark, joyless place.

He came from a loving, caring family – who were completely unaware of the pain he was experiencing. Paul, like most men, was a consummate actor when it came to hiding his emotions. Even his closest friends were unaware of how down he was.

He had learned early on that the only way to deal with the pain was to use alcohol as a crutch. With alcohol, his mood would lift briefly for a few hours and his friends would see the joker in him. The days following a binge would, however, lead to his mood dropping further, and often triggered further thoughts of suicide.

He was employed by an insurance company, and was adept at hiding his difficulties from his employers and work colleagues. No one realised how hard he had to work to carry out his day-to-day functions, due to fatigue and concentration difficulties. Paul was in a good relationship with his partner Sandra, who was also completely unaware of his underlying depression. She assumed at times when he seemed quiet that it was just his personality.

What nobody knew was that Paul, when he was nine, had been sexually abused by a good friend of the family. He had simply walled off that part of his life. He often considered the possibility that he might be suffering from depression but didn't want to go there.

Increasingly, the thought of suicide grew stronger, and the struggle to continue wore him down. He withdrew more into himself, and Sandra struggled to cope with the sudden change. She felt rejected, and reacted accordingly. The more she withdrew, the more Paul's depression deteriorated.

His work suffered, and his manager issued a verbal warning that he had to shape up. He spent more time in his room late at night on the internet. At weekends, he either avoided going out with his friends or ended up on a major binge.

Sandra eventually decided that they should take a break in their relationship to give her time to see how she felt. Paul agreed, and they split up. The last bulwark between Paul and suicide was now removed. The negative thinking that had dogged his life to date now took over with a vengeance:

- 'I understand why Sandra would leave me: I am worthless, useless and not deserving of her love. She can do much better.'
- 'I can't put up with this pain any longer.'
- 'I am such a burden on those who love me – particularly Sandra and my mum.'
- 'I crave peace!'
- 'Maybe it's time.'

The suicide thoughts transformed into planning. Paul researched relevant suicide websites. His main fear was that he would not be successful or, even worse that he might survive but be handicapped. Like most men, he was quite thorough in his preparations: nothing would be left to chance.

He set a date and spent the next few weeks meeting friends he was close to. He passed his favourite music collection on to his younger brother, who had always coveted it.

'I have grown out of it!'

His mood lifted as the weeks passed and the date grew closer. He spent as much time as possible with his mum in particular. He knew she would be upset but that it would be for the best: 'I won't be such a burden on her from now on.'

He felt a little guilty about Sandra. He arranged to meet her and they had a long conversation. He went out of his way to hide how he felt, or what his plans were. He even suggested that maybe they might get together at a later stage. Little did Sandra know, as they were embracing, that it could turn out to be for the last time.

Finally, the day arrived. He went to work as normal and carried out his usual functions. All his colleagues noted that he seemed in much better form.

He had already written his suicide notes to his family: 'I am sorry for all the pain I have caused you. It is for the best. I love you all.'

And also one to Sandra: 'I am sorry. Please forgive me. You deserve more. I love you. Goodbye. Paul.'

He left his workplace and drove to a lonely place where the pain would end. The river was deep and the currents swirled. He texted at the last minute to both his mum and Sandra: 'Goodbye, I love you.'

He stripped, left the suicide notes with his shoes and clothes, and jumped in.

But life, as always, stepped in to interfere with his plans. The sound of him entering the water alerted a man who had been hidden from view in a favourite fishing spot. He was an excellent swimmer and immediately dived in. By the time he got to Paul, Paul had already lost consciousness. His rescuer managed, with great difficulty, to pull him over to the riverside and then onto the bank. He did mouth-to-mouth resuscitation and alerted the emergency services on his mobile.

It was a really close call, but Paul survived, and woke up in Intensive Care. He was devastated that he had not been successful in his suicide attempt. His family, and Sandra, were outside, traumatised by what had happened. How could they not have recognised that Paul had been so distressed? Or that he would have gone to such extremes?

When Paul was recovering, he was overwhelmed with outpourings of love and empathy from his family, friends, and particularly Sandra. But that did not stop his mum from letting him know just how upset she was with him. Why had he had not opened up to her as to how he was feeling? Did he think so little of both his family and Sandra that he could not trust them to help him when he was in trouble?

The time in hospital gave Paul an opportunity to examine his life. Some good chats with the self-harm liaison nurse and visiting psychiatrist opened him up to the reality that he was suffering from depression.

The minute he was discharged from hospital, his mum brought him to see Dr Bill, the family doctor. This was to be a seminal moment. For the first time, Paul opened up to years of deep-seated emotional pain and despair. After some probing, Dr Bill even helped him acknowledge the abuse he had endured in his childhood.

By now, Paul had accepted that he was suffering from depression and was ready to start the journey back to recovery. The first step was to help him to start 'feeling better'.

They made a 'safety pact' in relation to further self-harm, and Dr Bill laid out a plan for the next eight weeks. Paul agreed to begin thirty minutes of exercise daily, even though he knew it would be a struggle due to fatigue. He also agreed to work with his mum in relation to a proper diet and to add B vitamins and Omega 3 fish oils to his daily regimen.

Paul would also take a period of time off work to deal with his depression. This would involve informing his workplace. To his surprise, his employers, aware now of what had happened, were incredibly supportive. He also agreed to cease alcohol for at least two months.

Finally, Paul would begin a course of modern antidepressants to help deal with the host of physical and psychological symptoms that had brought him to this dark place. The plan would be to carefully regulate these over the first few months and to dispense them on a weekly basis until Paul was back to himself.

Dr Bill explained that this would only be the second step on his road to recovery – the first being accepting his depression and coming for assistance. Later, they would examine the stress triggers, particularly the abusive background – but only when he was well enough to 'go there'.

Within four weeks, Paul was a little better and by eight weeks was, for the first time in a decade, feeling 'normal'. His energy and concentration were improving by the week, and he was sleeping and eating much better, thanks to his mother's cooking. He and Sandra were now back together and he found her to be a rock of strength. But Paul still has a long way to go on his journey.

We will follow his progress in future chapters.

## *Dr Bill's Comments*
We can learn much from Paul's story:

- It is very common for men, in particular, to hide their pain and deep-seated distress for many years. In many cases, they may never admit to anyone exactly how they are feeling.
- Men can be quite adept at concealing depression – so much so that it often comes as a major shock to family, friends and work colleagues if it comes to the surface. Remember, you can't see emotions!
- Men are actually hard-wired and culturally inured to blocking out and not expressing their emotions. This puts them at even more risk of serious self-harm if they are significantly depressed.
- If a man does make up his mind to take his own life, he will generally plan it with extreme care and thoroughness and as a result will often, unfortunately, be successful.
- Many will seem to improve in mood when they have decided to end it all. They will also quite commonly do a round of close friends and family to say 'goodbye' in their own minds.
- Some – particularly younger males – will give away prized possessions.
- Hidden abuse, often sexual in nature, can be the trigger for later depression in those who are susceptible to this illness. The internal self-loathing and guilt carried by men (and of course women) destroys their sense of self-worth, laying the groundwork for future disaster.
- Many men use alcohol as a way of numbing the pain of depression.
- Many men may end up breaking up relationships when they are very down, as they feel that they are 'not good enough' and that the girl 'could do a lot better'. I have seen this break up relationships, engagements and even marriages if the underlying depression is not identified, and help sought.

- Many men struggle to hold down jobs when they are depressed, due to the huge toll on their physical health, particularly in the areas of fatigue and concentration. Once again, they are adept at concealing this. However, sometimes it can come to a head as the employer may, without realising what is going on, rebuke the employee, assuming that they are simply not making the effort. This further reduces the person's self-esteem.

Paul saw no way out of the dark, cold world of pain and self-loathing, other than suicide. In his emotional distress, he felt that there were no other possible solutions to end the pain. However, as events unfolded after his lucky escape, he realised that there was another way to end his pain – and one which is not so traumatic for himself and his family.

Paul now realises what so many with depression who reach the stage of wanting to end it all, struggle to see – that they would only have passed the terrible burden of pain and suffering from themselves to those who love them.

This, for many families, is a lifetime sentence – with no parole.

## Claire's Story

Claire has suffered from anxiety since early childhood. Her mum told her jokingly that she was even anxious as a baby! She was similar to her father, who was quite a tense man. As a teenager, she was a constant worrier and perfectionist in relation to her appearance and school work. She was also sensitive to what others would say, although she often hid her upset. She struggled with the common symptoms of general anxiety, particularly fatigue, irritable bowel syndrome and tension headaches.

By her mid-twenties she has successfully completed her college and postgraduate studies. She was constantly encouraged by the love and support of her mum and always felt that she could share any of her difficulties with her. She met Tom, an easygoing teacher, and joined a company which recognised her dedication and perfectionism – and piled on the work!

Then things begin to take a turn for the worse. She finds her anxiety increasing and for the first time in her life develops panic attacks. The harder she tries to ensure that everything at work is perfect, the more fatigue she develops. Her sleep begins to become broken and she has constant nightmares of everything going wrong. Her concentration deteriorates, as does her appetite.

Then comes the major shock: her mum is diagnosed with breast cancer. Claire's world starts to collapse. She shared so much with her mum, and now that support was gone. Tom is very sympathetic, but it just isn't the same.

She begins to catastrophise that her mum is going to die. How would she cope if this happened? She spends as much time as possible with her mum, through the trauma of major surgery and radiotherapy. But her mother's illness begins to take its toll, and her mood plummets.

As her mood drops, her fatigue, concentration and appetite deteriorate further, as does her sleep. She starts to dread the panic attacks which come on her out of nowhere. Her employers, aware of her mother's illness, try to make allowances for her reduced work output but eventually put pressure on her to seek assistance. She talks to a work counsellor but doesn't explain exactly how badly she is feeling, for fear that it might damage work prospects.

Claire does not realise that she has slipped into a bout of major depression. She still feels that she is just anxious and needs to 'pull herself together'. But she is losing weight and has stopped enjoying anything in her life. She begins to push Tom away, feeling that he could do a lot better than being with a worthless person like her. Eventually, thoughts of self-harm begin to arrive; it is only the fact that her mum needs her support that stops her going down this road.

Luckily for Claire, her dad spots the drop in mood and sits her down for a good chat. He opens up about the fact that, over the years, he has had bouts of depression – most of which he tried to handle on his own. He had always asked his wife to keep this from his children, as he had felt ashamed of being seen to suffer from depression.

He admits that the turning point in his life was a referral by his family doctor to see Dr Bill for advice on how to deal with his depression. For Claire, the empathy bond created by this conversation bursts through the darkness, pain and self-loathing which had taken over her life. She no longer feels on her own, and realises that it is not anxiety that has been making her feel this way, but depression.

Together they attend Dr Bill and she explains how she has been feeling. It comes as a relief when he explains that her symptoms were due to a bout of depression. This had been brought on by battling with general anxiety for many years, and the major stress trigger of her mother's illness. When she reveals her thoughts of self-harm, she starts to cry, with a mixture of relief and shame.

Dr Bill explains that his first job is to try and help Claire feel better. The initial task is to help her, through a combination of lifestyle changes, drug therapy and support, get her life back into some semblance of order.

He lays out an exercise regimen of thirty minutes a day and they explore her nutrition. He adds supplements and is pleased that she is not using alcohol as a coping mechanism. He puts her on a course of drug therapy to try and help lift her mood, appetite, energy, sleep and concentration. Claire is terrified when she realises that she will have to go on to drug therapy: 'Aren't these drugs harmful, addictive and to be avoided at all costs? Will I be left on them for the rest of my life?'

Dr Bill treats her concerns seriously. Claire must be comfortable beginning such a course; otherwise, she would stop taking the medication inappropriately. He explains that, all going well, the course will last for around six to eight months, and they explore the pros and cons. He allays her fears and misconceptions and she agrees to begin drug therapy.

She looks for immediate help for the panic attacks, which have become such an issue in her life. He talks her through some simple CBT exercises to reduce these attacks.

They inform her employers as to what has been going on, and, with their support, she takes a six-week break from work. The plan is that when her physical and mood symptoms have improved, Claire will work with him to deal with the underlying anxiety plaguing her life.

After six weeks, Claire is feeling much better in terms of her mood, sleep, appetite, concentration and energy. The panic attacks have receded. She is now ready to move on to the next step: getting better. Later we will see how she gets on.

*Dr Bill's Comments*
We can learn much from Claire's story:

- It is common for anxiety to be a trigger for developing major depression at some stage in our lives.
- Although in the vast majority of cases panic attacks occur on their own, or are associated with general anxiety, they can, on occasion, be triggered or worsened by depression itself.
- It is often a major stress trigger, such as in Claire's case her mum's illness, that sets off a bout of depression.
- Once the bout begins, it usually takes on a life of its own, irrespective of the stress trigger which precipitated it.
- Many people with depression fail to realise that the physical symptoms they are experiencing – particularly difficulties with energy, sleep, appetite and concentration – are warning signs of the illness.
- Significant thoughts of self-harm are usually another warning sign of depression.
- It is very common for depression to follow on in families, so never be afraid to ask parents if it has been an issue in their lives.
- There are many misconceptions about the role of drug therapy in the general community: antidepressants are not the answer to life's problems but play a key role in helping us feel better, as part of a holistic package.
- A holistic package can quickly get us back feeling better, and back in control of our own lives.
- Many people struggle on for months, even years, feeling terrible and never realising that there is a much easier way of dealing with these debilitating symptoms.

## Peter's Story

Peter is in his late thirties. His first encounter with depression was in his early twenties when he was at college: he got through this period with the assistance of a college counsellor. He has a good job in a company which had boomed during the Celtic Tiger era. Like many in modern Ireland, he fell into the trap of taking out a high mortgage, together with his partner Marie.

They had two children, Nessa and John.

Then the bubble burst and he was put under protective notice. His partner's hours were also cut. Money began to dry up and Peter found himself becoming increasingly stressed. The banks began to put pressure on in terms of repaying personal loans; the letters and phone calls never seemed to stop. This led to constant arguments as to how they could cut costs further in the house.

Then the news they had been dreading finally arrived. The company had gone into liquidation and Peter would only receive statutory redundancy. While they could use this to make some dent in their mortgage arrears , they would still be in serious financial difficulties.

Peter's mood started to plummet. His 'internal critic' began to take over. He felt useless as a father, a partner and a provider for his family. He stopped answering the phone or opening letters from the bank. He became more withdrawn and stopped exercising. He stayed up late at night aimlessly trawling the internet searching for some way out of his dilemma. He started to feel exhausted and hopeless, and struggled to get out of bed in the morning.

He ended up withdrawing more and more from Marie, and his libido dropped. He started to drink more, mainly at home, but felt worse the following day.

He began to check up on his life insurance policy, trying to see if there might be another way of salvaging Marie and the children. He began to feel increasingly hopeless and worthless. His overriding emotions, apart from depression, were shame and guilt.

Sometimes, when the children were at school and Marie was at work, he would go off in the car so that neighbours would think that he was at work. Increasingly, he found himself when out driving wondering how he could set up his own death as a road traffic accident.

He concealed how he felt from Marie and other family members, who were concerned that he seemed to be withdrawing into himself. Everybody was afraid to approach him in case they would say the wrong thing and make matters worse.

Peter's mood deteriorated to a point where he couldn't go on. All he could see was the darkness, the pain and the isolation: 'There is no hope!'

It was his youngest child Nessa who saved him. He had decided after a long period of investigation on the web as to how best to solve the problem by removing himself from the equation.

But on the evening before, Nessa, with the instinctive love and trust of a child, comes over to him and hops up into his lap. She hugs him tightly and declares: 'I love you so much, Daddy.'

Peter suddenly finds himself in floods of tears. How could he just leave Nessa, who loved him so much? There had to be another way. Later, he decides to ring a depression helpline, whose number he had come across on the web. It was to be a life-changing conversation, as he realised that there were countless others experiencing the same symptoms and emotions as him. They advised him to open up to somebody close to him and to attend his family doctor or a therapist.

He decides to open up to Marie about how he was truly feeling, even though he found this to be one of the hardest things he had ever done. They both cried as he admitted how close he had come to ending it all. She exclaimed: 'I would have died inside without you: the pain would never have left!'

All the pain, hopelessness and feelings of worthlessness just burst out of him, and he felt a great sense of relief. He also felt that whatever had to be done to get better, they would do it together.

They decide that, together, they would attend Dr Bill and seek assistance for Peter's depression. He finds it easier to have Marie with him for the first visit and opens up to Dr Bill about the way he has been feeling emotionally and physically. He explains that Peter has been experiencing the classical symptoms of depression, driven by the massive stress of losing his job and by the twin demons of guilt and shame, which so often accompany the latter.

Dr Bill then sets out a new path to deal with his depression. He suggests that Peter start thirty minutes of exercise a day. He gets him to avoid alcohol and they examine his diet. Peter is initially unhappy with the thought of using medication to try and lift his mood and deal with his physical symptoms. Dr Bill asks him: 'Would you have the same problems if I were putting you on medication for a condition like diabetes?'

Dr Bill goes on to explain all the links between the various physical illnesses, like diabetes, coronary heart disease and depression. Peter realises that this illness is actually far more physical than he appreciated. With Marie's encouragement, he agrees to give it a trial. 'Anything is better than the world I have been living in,' he admits.

Dr Bill arranges to see him regularly over the next six to eight weeks, as he is concerned about just how low Peter's mood has fallen. Peter finds his support, and that of his wife, invaluable during this period.

They agree that once this part of the journey is over and he is feeling well enough, they will deal with the various stress issues which had triggered the bout of depression. As a temporary measure, Dr Bill gives him a letter to his bank asking them for some leeway to deal with the issues in question. To Peter's surprise, once they realised that he had become extremely depressed as a result of all that had happened, they ended their relentless barrage of him.

Later, we will see how Peter deals with the emotions of guilt and shame that had come so close to causing his family lifelong heartbreak.

### Dr Bill's Comments

One of the commonest stress triggers for developing a bout of major depression in today's Ireland is the devastating trio of job loss, personal debt and negative equity.

Men in particular struggle to deal with the emotional maelstrom that this trio can create.

Guilt and shame are the emotions that are usually triggered, along with the normal feelings of anxiety that anyone would experience in such situations.

In those who are vulnerable to depression, these two emotions can trigger a bout of the illness.

If this happens, the person's nightmare gets worse, as they experience the physical and psychological impact of depression itself.

The trio of guilt, shame and depression leads to a complete breakdown in the person's self-worth, and they are at greater risk of self-harm if they do not seek help.

Sometimes it can be the simple, pure love of a child or somebody close to us that stands in the way of this becoming a reality.

Peter recognises almost too late just how devastating it would have been for his partner and children if he had gone through with his plans.

When we are very down, we can see no way out of the dark world we are inhabiting, but with good professional help and the love of those close to us, we can get through it.

It is very important for men in particular to realise that depression is just as much a physical illness as heart disease and diabetes, and must be treated as such, with lifestyle changes, drug therapy and counselling being used as necessary in each case.

It is not wise to try and deal immediately with the stress triggers and negative emotions like guilt and shame, but better to use a holistic approach to start feeling better first and then move on to deal with such issues.

## Christina's Story

Christina had experienced depression throughout her adult life; it had visited her for the first time at the age of nineteen. She came from a family background steeped in the illness, so it was no surprise that she too developed it.

She had been shaped by the experiences of seeing her mum and dad battle with depression during her childhood and early teens. It was Christina who had found her mum unconscious following a serious overdose of tablets, and this episode left an indelible mark.

She was now in her mid-thirties and struggling. She was extremely bright and was managing to hold down her job as a teacher, albeit with some difficulty. Christina over the years had become socially isolated. She had been in a number of good relationships but would keep breaking them off. She always felt that the men in question deserved somebody better. Her world was narrowing down to a daily battle to get up, carry out her normal domestic chores and deal with her teaching post.

Over the years she had approached doctors and therapists for assistance but was never able to lift the pall for any period. She had taken a number of courses of antidepressants but could never tolerate them for more than a few weeks before throwing them away. She could never shake off the memory of her own mum and how she became almost zombie-like on the medication prescribed by her psychiatrist.

Christina had a pathological fear of both antidepressants and psychiatrists. She had vowed to never go down that road, no matter how difficult things became. Instead, she spent fruitless years going down the alternative/complementary road – and spent a fortune with countless such therapists, all promising a quick fix. Unfortunately none of them worked and she was now getting desperate.

Matters come to a head when she does badly in an impromptu school inspection. Her principal, who has been concerned about her for some time, decides to come and see her. Christina ends up breaking down in tears and opens up to the pain and blackness within her. The principal is extremely empathetic and asks her if she would like to attend Dr Bill. The principal admits to Christina that she herself had gone through a period of recurrent panic attacks and had found him very helpful. She persuades Christina to take an extended break from work to get help for her depression.

Christina comes to see Dr Bill and finds him very easy to open up to. She details the many and varied therapies she has tried over the years. She also expresses her difficulties with many of the modern antidepressants, and how she felt she would never feel 'normal' again. He explains the holistic approach to depression, and she is agreeable to the various lifestyle changes suggested. She admits to struggling with exercise but promises to try. She also agrees to cease alcohol, on which she had become increasingly dependent.

Dr Bill decides to try her on an old-fashioned antidepressant. He explains that a small number of people do not tolerate the modern forms and often respond to older types. She also agrees not to try any alternative therapies until she has given his approach time to work.

Dr Bill sees Christina regularly over the next six to eight weeks, and she remains off work during this period. To her surprise, her mood, sleep, energy and appetite all improve, and she begins to feel better than she has in years. But she is still plagued with constant internal ruminations, which make her feel worthless. At least now she is ready to move on the next phase of talk therapy, aimed at helping her to 'get better'. We will rejoin her later.

*Dr Bill's Comments*

Christina belongs to a smaller group of the population who suffer continuous bouts of depression.

It is common in such cases to have a strong family history of major depression in parents and siblings.

Many people spend large amounts of money and time travelling down alternative routes to treating depression, which end up in a dead-end.

We now know that for multiple reasons (many of which may be genetic in nature), people will respond differently to antidepressants, both old and new.

If the person is struggling with the physical and psychological symptoms of depression, it is worth persevering in such cases until a suitable one is found.

A period off work, if trying to apply a holistic therapy approach, can in some cases take the pressure off the person, allowing them to work on all the lifestyle changes necessary.

Even if drug therapy has been successful in helping the person improve physically, they will still have work to do to learn to deal with the negative thoughts, feelings of worthlessness, and constant rumination so prevalent in this illness.

This is where talk therapy comes into its own – as we will now examine.

# PART FIVE

## Step Three (2 to 8 months)
## How To Get Better!

I hope that by now you are feeling better in terms of mood, energy, drive, sleep and appetite. If not, revert back to Step Two and keep working with the professional guide you have chosen. If you try to move on to Step Three and are still struggling with energy and concentration, you will find it extremely difficult. I will assume that, if you are reading on, you are feeling better and are ready to continue.

The period between two and four months is crucial. Many assume that, as they are feeling better, their depression has now been treated. As a result, they may cease the crucial lifestyle changes they have implemented, stop their drug therapy (if they are on it) or detach from the professional doctor or therapist they have been dealing with. Unfortunately, this can lead to the depression bout returning.

Although you may be feeling better physically and mood-wise, there is more to be done regarding your thinking and behaviour. This may involve assessing stress triggers that are causing problems in the present, or it may involve dealing with difficulties which have arisen in the past relating to issues like guilt, hurt, nonvalidating environments and abuse. Without doing this, you may not get to the heart of your particular difficulties. For everyone, this journey will differ. But all must travel it if they want to get better.

Step Three will involve:

- Continuing the holistic approach involving lifestyle changes and drug therapy (if relevant) started in Step Two.
- Analysing major stress triggers which may have led to the arrival of this particular bout of depression in your life.
- Learning new skills to help deal with the negative thinking, constant rumination and unhealthy behaviour patterns so prevalent in depression.
- Examining the possibility of counselling or therapy if there are issues in relation to grief, abuse, significant difficulties in our past, addiction, major traumas, and so on.
- If we suffer from significant bouts of anxiety in between bouts of depression, or are carrying around major negative emotions like shame, guilt or hurt – using the various forms of talk therapy like CBT to help us deal with them.

All of these are full of pitfalls that many may not recognise.

## Continuing The Holistic Approach, Involving Lifestyle Changes And Drug Therapy (If Relevant), Started In Step Two

This is the first hurdle, and many people stumble. It is essential to continue the lifestyle and drug therapy (if relevant) approach that has got you feeling better.

### Lifestyle Changes

It is important to keep up thirty minutes of daily exercise, no matter how difficult you find this. So many become lazy about this and will feel their mood slipping as a result. It is also important to keep up a healthy diet and to take Omega 3 and B complex supplements.

Alcohol is another potential pitfall. You may have abstained for the first few months as you were initially feeling so poorly. But once you are feeling better you may be tempted to restart. It is important to remain 'self-aware' of alcohol's potential effects on mood in particular. If you find your mood dropping following a bout of drinking, consider ceasing it for another while.

It is important to keep to a regular daily routine – as much as is possible within the parameters of modern busy lives. Try and avoid going for long naps during the day, no matter how tired you feel. It has been shown scientifically that our mood often deteriorates after these: our serotonin mood cable in the brain switches off when we are asleep. Sleep is a key factor in keeping physically and mentally well, but it should be confined to a regular eight-hour period at night. If you are feeling tired during the daytime, do thirty minutes of exercise instead; this will greatly reduce these symptoms.

When people with depression allow their lifestyle to spiral out of control, sleep is one of the first things to suffer. Many will trace relapses back to their sleep cycle getting out of sync. If you are having specific problems with this, discuss them with your family doctor. Also, if you are using light therapy, in the form of a dawn simulator or a light-box, continue using this therapy.

## Drug Therapy

This is one of the commonest problem areas at this stage in the healing process. Around two to three months into a holistic package including antidepressants, we are usually feeling much better.

This, paradoxically, is when problems can ensue. Many assume that because they are now feeling well, they should cease drug therapy. The reasons for this are numerous but the following are typical thoughts that can lead to it happening:

- 'I am feeling so well: I no longer need medication to stay that way!'
- 'My family and partner are not happy with me being on antidepressants. Now I feel better, it would be best if I stopped them.'
- 'I'd better stop – before I become addicted.'
- 'Maybe my sex drive might improve if I come off them. I'm reaching a point where I feel interested in sex again.'
- 'I have felt so ashamed and weak at having to take medication for "depression".'
- 'I now feel that I can do this on my own: I don't need tablets!'
- 'I know so many people who have been on them for long periods. I am not going down that road. It would be best if I stopped them now.'
- 'Worst of all, these tablets must be changing "me" the person. This truly

frightens me! It's best to cease before I am irrevocably changed!'

So is three months the right time to stop antidepressants? In practice, this does not seem to work. It is the experience of many professionals that patients' depression may begin again, usually within four to six weeks. It is important to realise that these drugs have both a short- and long-term action. The former helps our mood improve, and physical symptoms like sleep, appetite, drive and concentration to settle. This helps us feel better, usually within two months. This mainly happens by means of the drug therapy acting on our emotional brain and mood cables.

There is, however, a longer-acting effect which can take up to six months; this occurs higher up in our logical brain. It is this effect that helps us get better.

The thoughts expressed above are so incredibly common, however, that many people chance stopping their drug therapy at two to three months. Many of the ideas expressed are of course inaccurate.

For example, how could taking a drug therapy for an illness make you 'weak' or give rise to an emotion like shame? Many assume that they will become addicted, but in practice this is not so. If you are in the middle of a proper holistic therapy regimen, you will probably be off them after nine to ten months. It is sad that family pressure (often from well-meaning but misguided spouses) is one of the commonest reasons for people to cease drug therapy at this two- to three-month phase. The family member often feels ashamed that somebody they love and live with should be 'so weak' mentally as to require medication. This may or not be directly expressed, but the person with depression will be picking up these negative thoughts and respond by stopping taking their tablets. This leads to an inevitable downwards spiral. The person stops medication and their mood drops; this isolates them further from those they love. The latter points to this drop in mood as a clear indication that the person with depression is dependent on the drug. This leads to further pressure on the person to stay off the drugs, and the depression recurs.

Sex is another important area. Most people with major depression have an almost complete lack of sexual drive and libido. Sex is the last thing on their mind: their survival is of greater importance. This leads to all kinds of difficulties with spouses and partners who don't understand the world the person with depression is living in.

But as they start to feel better, their sex drive and libido improves. Some of the modern antidepressants can make sex drive and orgasm more difficult for some men and women. This can be very frustrating for both them and their partners. This side effect can vary greatly from person to person. But unilaterally stopping medication will not solve the problem, as the depression may relapse, and with it any interest in sex at all! It is better to complete the course laid out by your doctor and see if anything can be done to assist in this area until the course has been completed. The good news is that any sexual difficulties associated with antidepressants are usually gone within seven to ten days after stopping medication.

One of the most subtle and yet devastating negative thoughts around this phase is that antidepressants are 'altering me the person' and that 'I might never get back to being the person I really am!' This of course is completely untrue, but it is a powerful negative thought and leads many to cease taking medication. Would we say the same if we were taking a drug for Parkinson's disease or diabetes? This shows how far we have to travel to help people understand that depression is in part a physical illness and that the drugs do *not* change who we are as people.

I appeal to all those accompanying us on the journey to stay the course in relation to drug therapy. Nobody likes to be on medication for any illness, and depression is no different. The great advantage of depression over other illnesses is that in the main we will only have to take a course for nine months.

If you are prepared to do so, and to continue with your lifestyle changes, the benefits that will accrue are significant.

## How To Analyse The Major Stress Triggers Which Led To The Arrival Of This Particular Bout Of Depression

It has been recognised for over a hundred years that the commonest trigger for a bout of major depression is a period of significant stress. As we have emerged into the twenty-first century with our new understanding of the neuroscience underlying this condition, we understand why. Some become confused, in that stress in certain situations is seen as the *cause* of the bout of depression in question. Stress is *not* the cause of depression: rather, it is the *trigger* which set off the bout. Many of us experience long bouts of significant stress but do not develop major depression. Some seem more resilient, through genes and upbringing, in coping with stress. Others, prone to become more anxious and fretful when exposed to significant stress, may proceed to depression.

If feeling better, it is time to analyse any stress triggers that may have set off this particular bout of depression. This is best done with a pen and paper, and preferably with the help of your guide, whether doctor or therapist.

Although some stressors have their origins in the past, we will confine ourselves in this section to *immediate stressors*.

## Financial Difficulties

These can be a major stress trigger leading to major depression.

As long as human beings exist, there will always be challenges when it comes to providing the necessities of life for ourselves and our families. When times are difficult, the stress to provide enough funds to meet this challenge can be a constant, daily battle.

If you have become depressed from coping with a prolonged spell of such pressure, then read on! If feeling better, this is the time for a radical overhaul of personal and family finances.

Many end up with different loans from varied sources. In some cases, debt problems become so severe that official and unofficial moneylenders become involved. The latter is a real recipe for disaster!

Groups like MABS are extremely effective at helping us work out a strategy to deal with our particular situation. They will come up with a planned package and can mediate between you and financial institutions. Others may prefer to work with a personal financial advisor to do the same.

It is vital to deal with such issues, which you may have being trying to avoid. Often what seem like insurmountable obstacles can be overcome with the help of others.

Above all, stay out of the hands of moneylenders or those who would use your financial weakness as a means of making large profits. Also, never let banks or financial institutions bully you. There are a whole host of bodies such as MABS who can act as buffers in such situations.

Often making a simple list of the five main financial problem areas, and working with experts in the area, can transform this stress trigger.

One word of caution to men is to avoid at all costs the world of shame. Many feel ashamed if financial difficulties are causing distress to their families. Remember that in many cases, financial difficulties arise due to circumstances outside our control. So it is the *situation* which is abnormal, not us! Men often struggle to realise this – and to express the pressure they are feeling – and so remain more at risk.

If you want to truly get the better of depression, you must deal with any major financial difficulties in your life. Otherwise these difficulties will drag down your mood again at a later stage.

## Relationship Difficulties

These are perhaps the most powerful stress trigger which can set off a bout of depression. This is understandable, as our emotional brain is so strong, and relationships are at their heart 'emotional' in nature.

There are many different types of relationships in our everyday lives. The ones giving rise to the greatest difficulties are those between partners or spouses, and between parents and children.

The depth of emotion that underlies relationships between men and women (and obviously in same-sex relationships too) can be incredibly powerful, both in a positive sense when things are going well, and in a destructive sense when they are not!

We live in a modern society that is experiencing breakdowns of many structures and belief systems. It is not surprising that many relationships are getting into difficulties. Many couples struggle with constant financial and housing difficulties, which can lead to rows and strife. Some relationships also struggle to deal with the stresses involved in rearing children in this modern cauldron.

There can also be significant difficulties if there is an imbalance within relationships. In some cases, one side may be more interested in, or attracted to, their partner than the reverse. This can lead to tension and breakdowns in relationships. We see this regularly among young boys and girls in their late teens and twenties in particular, and it can lead to significant depression in those vulnerable to the condition.

We are also seeing a lot of relationships breaking down among people in their thirties, forties and fifties. The reasons for this are also myriad, but in many cases the couple have just drifted apart.

If problems with personal relationships have been the major stress trigger which set off your particular bout of depression, what can you do? The first thing is to get out a sheet of paper and document the main problem areas:

- Is it a good relationship at all?
- Is it only in trouble because you have been depressed or has it been in difficulty for quite some time?
- Do you love the person?
- Do you honestly feel that they love you?
- What do you feel the major hurdles are in the relationship?
- Can you sort them out with your partner, now that you are feeling better?
- Would couple counselling help and, if so, would your partner agree to attend?
- Are the main problems financial or housing issues? If so, would seeking out help with these sort out the main problems?
- Are the difficulties between you due more to issues with in-laws rather than between yourselves?
- Would it be healthier for both sides to break up the relationship if they are in real difficulties?

These are the questions we may end up having to ask. It is hard to do this on your own, and beneficial to work with a counsellor or therapist (either on your own or, ideally, together with your partner) if you want to sort things out.

Sometimes a frank listing of the problems and a good chat with our partner may be all that is required. It would be my experience that many, when 'feeling better' in relation to their depression, are well able to sort out matters themselves. But there will be more complex situations when outside help is advisable.

The key word is 'honesty', for too many play emotional mind games with themselves and others. They are not being honest with their own emotions, as they fear loss of the relationship above all else. This can lead to self-destruction in terms of depression, as the problems will not just go away: they have to be faced down and dealt with.

Relationship difficulties occur between parents and children at every stage of life. Many assume that we are only talking about that normal traumatic phase between twelve and twenty, but these problems can also arise much later in life.

It is inevitable that the teenage years and early twenties are often a very trying time for both parents and children. Some children and young adults will come from difficult abusive, addictive or violent backgrounds, and relationships with their parents may be fraught for life as a result. In other situations, the child is reared in what they feel is an emotionally non-validating environment. They carry hurt or a chip on their shoulder into their adult life. This can lead to rows and estrangement from parents as time goes on.

There can also be major sibling rivalry within families that can tear them apart. As parents age and require more support from offspring, tensions can arise. This can lead to significant stress, and in some cases depression.

Such issues can be very complex. If you feel that there is stress coming from this area, you must deal with it. Again, a list of the main concerns can be very helpful. You can then either work together with other members of your family or with your parents or children to see if problems can be worked out. Once again, some counselling or therapy, either personally or as a group, can be helpful.

## Work Difficulties

These are another important stress trigger for a bout of depression. Here are four issues that constantly give rise to difficulty.

The first relates to work bullying. This can be devastating, and even fatal, for some people who are prone to depression. The bullying can either be from management to staff or between fellow workers. It can sometimes be overt but more often subtle and nasty. It can, on occasion, be sexual in nature. The concern is that people are now so vulnerable in terms of holding down jobs that they are afraid to rock the boat and approach relevant authorities.

For the person with depression, bullying only confirms what they in their own internal emotional world have already decided: that they are of no worth and deserve to be treated in such a way. Some will experience a profound loss of self-dignity and self-worth and feel that self-harm is the only way to deal with the problem. Many with depression will end up in a vicious circle. The more they are bullied, the more stressed they get; this in turn leads to further drops in mood; this leads to poorer work performance; which leaves them open to even more taunts and bullying. If the bullying also involves dumping of excessive amounts of work on the victim, then the situation will get worse, as the person with depression is already struggling.

One useful tip is to explain what has been going on to your doctor and seek his or her help. He or she will usually put you off work and write to your personnel department or boss detailing his or her concerns about your work situation. It is also useful to attend talk therapy to learn skills as to how to deal with bullies. Often a sensible mix of these measures can lead to a major reduction in stress brought on by bullying at work. In very extreme situations, legal assistance and advice can be sought, as can the involvement of relevant unions.

Remember, it is the bully and the situation which are abnormal, not you! The biggest mistake occurs when employees do not admit to what is going on in the workplace. This feeds the bully, who can work away uninhibited. So you must face (with help) your enemy. You will be surprised by just how quickly bullies run for cover when they are faced down!

The second relates to an increasing problem where fewer and fewer people employed are being asked to do more and more. While this is fine if the employee is extremely resilient physically and mentally, the rest (who form the majority) may struggle.

The employer in question is not trying to create difficulties. They are trying to cut corners to increase profits and survive. They may be unaware of how much stress is being heaped on their employees' shoulders. Some just can't cope with this increased workload and become toxically stressed and, if vulnerable, seriously depressed. Once again, if this was your stress trigger, open up to your doctor, therapist and, in particular, your boss. This, plus counselling if it is felt necessary, can lead to a major improvement in the work situation, with employers hopefully becoming more realistic about what is actually possible.

The third big stress trigger for many at work is the fear that they will lose their job. This is because of negative media coverage of the crisis and the reality that many businesses are struggling to survive. Many become so anxious or stressed at even the thought that they might lose their job that they eventually become depressed. They become as worried about the possibility of losing their job as they would have been if this had actually happened.

If this is an issue, then document what evidence there is to back up your assertions. Our worst fears generally do not materialise, but in our emotional minds they already have!

Later we will be showing how simple CBT concepts can help us challenge this false assumption. You must learn to challenge this assumption. Otherwise, your depression is likely to recur. Again, some sessions with a CBT therapist can assist us in dealing with this anxiety.

Lastly, there is the obvious trigger of actually losing your job. This can be a devastating experience for even the most resilient. In particular, men in their middle years really struggle, as they are aware that their chances of finding further employment are slim. For them, their whole reason for existence implodes. They are hit with the twin problems of losing financial security and the social structure built around their workplace.

Unemployment, in all its forms and at every stage of life, is devastating. Some from disadvantaged areas may never find employment, and the loss of self-esteem that ensues drives many into the worlds of addiction and depression. For those who have been fortunate to have been employed, the loss of a job is a major challenge, whatever their age. There are practical things we can do to deal with the negative emotions that unemployment brings:

- Try and maintain a regular routine as if you are still employed.
- Try and exercise regularly.

- Do as many training modules as you can.
- If you cannot find work no matter how hard you try, then give your skills to some community projects on a voluntary basis.
- If you are under thirty and free to travel, then consider taking a few years out to travel to somewhere where you might find work.
- Remember, 'work is not worth'! We are so much more than our jobs.
- We are so important to those around us – whether it be fathers, mothers, sons, daughters and friends. None of these require us to be employed!
- Work hard at maintaining the social relationships that have been created with workmates.

## Sexual Identity Difficulties

These are another common stress trigger for depression. For many young males in particular, it can be difficult to come to terms with their sexuality. If the person is clearly gay, then there may be concerns about whether or not to open up to family or loved ones. Many older men and women may also be in marriages where they feel trapped. This gives rise to feelings of shame, guilt, anger, anxiety and, in those who are vulnerable, depression.

Younger age groups may be unsure as to their sexuality, and this too can give rise to significant stress and depression. Some will be so emotionally traumatised and depressed that suicide may seem like the only way out of the problem. This can be a particular risk if sexual bullying at school or work occurs.

If these have been significant contributors to the stress which brought on this bout of depression, it is crucial that you face this issue. You should talk through the issues with a counsellor versed in helping people come to terms with their sexuality. If they feel that it is appropriate for you to disclose your sexuality to those you love, it might be healthier to let them know where you stand, even if this is difficult.

## Housing Difficulties

These are fast becoming another major stress trigger. Many are in negative equity and struggling to pay their mortgages each month. They are continually harassed and live in constant dread of being dumped out on the streets by uncaring institutions and banks.

Many put their heads in the sand and don't restructure their mortgage repayments with banks in time, allowing the situation to get out of control. Others are trapped in unsuitable accommodation and don't know how to get around the problem. Others are unable to get started on the housing ladder at all.

The key is accepting that you can only do what you can. It is vital that you interface with the financial institutions, either on your own or, if possible, with professional help, to reduce the stress involved. If this has been the big stressor triggering your bout of depression, then you must deal with it using whatever means are at your disposal.

The above are only a sample of the many and varied stress triggers which may lead us into the world of depression. The approach should always be the same, no matter what the stressor. We must identify the problem, write out what you feel are the main issues, and seek help in the form of counselling, therapy, financial and mortgage advice, and so on. We then try as best we can to reduce the risk of these being an ongoing stress trigger that might bring down our mood at a later date.

## Examining The Possibility Of Counselling Or Therapy If There Are Issues In Relation To Grief, Abuse, Non-Validating Environments, Addiction Or Major Trauma

Whilst the last section dealt with *current* everyday stress triggers for depression, this one deals with the past. It also deals with abuse, addiction, trauma and grief. If you feel that this is not of relevance to you personally, then move on to the next section. If you feel that it is, read on.

Many end up carrying deep-seated emotional scars from the past. These may have occurred during their upbringing, and some are extremely traumatised by them. Let's examine a few of the most common.

### Abuse

Abuse in all its forms is one of the most destructive occurrences in a person's life. The horror of sexual abuse of young children and teenagers can leave them scarred, emotionally, sexually and physically, for life. We now know, for example, that the memory box in our emotional brain can be so damaged by this act that in some it has shrunk in size on the right-hand side of the brain as adults.

While most adults seem to be able to put to one side physical abuse and a lack of emotional nourishment, few can deal with significant sexual abuse or rape as children. In many cases, the person has never admitted the presence of rape to parents or other family members or friends. They have locked it away in their unconscious emotional brain, where the hurt, anxiety, suppressed anger and shame eat away at their soul. It is inevitable that in those at risk, it leads in adult life to recurrent, and sometimes severe, bouts of depression.

Many who develop depression may accept help for their illness but never open up to this monster within. Because of this, it can be extremely difficult for them to receive long-term help. Some feel that they deserved to be abused or that something about them led the abuser to act in the way they did. Others carry huge hurt and anger towards those who were their protectors (often one or other parent). They may have sought help at the time to stop their abuse but their voices were ignored.

They can in such situations be extremely hurt that they were neither heard nor validated.

If you are reading this and it is striking a chord, then now is the time to finally deal with such abuse. You first of all have to accept that if it happened, you must open up to your guide, doctor or therapist about what occurred. This could be the most important step you will take in terms of your mental health. You cannot leave this inner wound to fester, poison and emotionally kill your soul. It can be both incredibly traumatic and yet liberating to take this step – but one you will never regret.

If it is now on the table, you must get professional counselling or therapy, either with a group like RIAN or with therapists skilled in this area. If you begin this work and struggle to deal with emotions like hurt, then a senior CBT therapist can be of enormous help.

Learning to come to terms with abuse can take a lot of work with a therapist but will lead you to a new space. It will also make it easier both to get better from major depression and to stay well.

## Grief

Grief is a completely normal, healthy emotion felt by us all at the loss of loved ones, whether they be family, spouses, children, siblings or close friends. Most can deal with it on their own with the support of friends and loved ones; others may need some bereavement counselling to help them move on.

However, it is now recognised that we can develop a more severe form of grief called pathological grief. This is where the loss is so severely felt by the person that they become literally stuck emotionally, and some develop severe depression as a consequence. They can continue in this state for long periods, even years.

Many will feel that they have actually grieved but are still stuck in the first stage of grief: a state of denial. The depression bout may arrive much later, and nobody connects the two happenings.

So if you can relate to this, it is vital that, if feeling better, you revisit grief. You may need to get counselling to air your emotions and thoughts about the death, and grieve properly. If you do, you may find your depression getting better and hopefully not recurring.

## Major Trauma

This can be another hidden trigger for depression bouts. Many of us experience significant major trauma throughout our lives and don't take into account the emotional consequences that can occur long after it happens.

Children who lose parents or siblings through serious illnesses, accidents and suicide can lock up these negative emotional experiences in their emotional brain and carry them into adult life. So, too, adults who have been in serious car crashes or who have had brushes with death for any reason, or have lost somebody close to them through accident or suicide, can also be extremely traumatised.

In such cases, the person may at a later stage suffer from anxiety, panic attacks and, if vulnerable, to bouts of major depression. Many never connect the dots and fail to see that they need to deal with the effects of such traumas in their emotional lives. Otherwise, the consequences may lead to recurrent bouts of depression.

If you can relate to any of these, you may be suffering from some post-traumatic stress disorder symptoms and will need counselling or CBT to help you come to terms with what has happened to you in the past. Once again, please open up to your guide if you feel that the above is relevant to you.

## Addiction

Addiction is another powerful stress trigger for developing major depression. Personal addiction or abuse in the form of alcohol or drugs (illegal and pre-scribed), gambling and the internet can be major triggers for depression in those who are vulnerable. Many fail either to accept this or to seek help.

There is a significant problem in modern Ireland with what is called Dual Diagnosis. This relates to having both major depression and an addiction (or addictions) to, in particular, alcohol, but in other situations drugs or gambling. It poses a major diagnostic and treatment challenge for both the doctor or therapist and the person in question.

If the sufferer openly admits to having an addictive problem and is prepared to attend individual and group therapy, then there can be a good result. The problem is that many deny that they have addictive problems but still want their depression treated and their lives returned to normal.

If you can relate to this and have not informed those who are caring for you, then it will be difficult, if not impossible, to help you get better and stay well.

On the other hand, if you come forward for help and use self-help groups like AA to help treat your depression, the future looks brighter. The choice is yours! I have seen many lives changed utterly by people turning to face their demons in this area, and also receiving help for their depression.

The second big group affected by depression and addiction is made up of those who have been reared by or are living with people with chronic alcohol or drug addiction. This group, like those who were abused, also grew up feeling that they were in some way responsible for their father's or mother's drinking.

The adult children of alcoholics, for example, are a classical example of those who have been hurt by addiction. But it includes spouses, siblings and all those close to the person with the addiction.

The consequences of learning to live with the addict's 'defensive wall' (see *Flagging the Problem*) of lies, minimising problems, stealing and being made to feel that they were in some way responsible for the person's addiction, are often buried away in the emotional brain. If not recognised and dealt with, they can lead to anxiety, panic attacks and depression.

If you can relate to this, I strongly recommend that you open up to your guide about this area and start attending one of the many excellent self-help groups, like Alanon, to learn how to detach and deal with the addict wall. In some cases, attending an alcohol counsellor will be of assistance. If you need to deal with emotional hurt from the past, then working with a therapist can help you develop the necessary skills.

In all of these situations, unless you are brutally honest as to the effects of addiction in your life, either directly or indirectly, then treating our depression is going to be more difficult.

## Non-Validating Environments

These are another common predisposing stress trigger in our past and present lives. This is where we grow up, or live at the moment, in an environment where our emotions are either completely ignored or swept aside if expressed.

We all need the emotional nourishment of our feelings being heard and, more importantly, validated. Many children grow up in houses where neither happens. Their emotional and psychological growth can become stunted, as can their sense of self-worth.

Others may live in the present, where once again they are not allowed to express how they feel and are mocked or ignored when they do. The consequences in both situations can be lifelong if they are not recognised and dealt with. The subject is brilliantly dealt with by my colleague, the superb therapist Enda Murphy, in a new book soon to be published.

Enda makes the point that in some cases we move on from such non-validating environments in our past to developing our own internal 'pathological critic'. This continues the relentless 'self-downing' the person experienced as a child.

This can act as a powerful trigger to set off a bout of depression. Once this happens, the internal pathological critic goes wild. We end up with a non-stop internal dialogue of self-hatred and criticism.

Many will ask: what is the point in focusing on such a nonvalidating environment, as most of this occurred in the past and there is little we can do about it now? While this is a reasonable stand to take, it fails to take into account the damage being done in the here and now. If we believe the nonsense which our internal pathological critic feeds us, it will be difficult to achieve our objective of getting better and staying well.

This is where talk therapy can be such a powerful tool. With the help of CBT skills in particular, we can learn to challenge our internal critic and overcome obstacles that non-validating environments create.

### Learning New Skills To Help Deal With The Negative Thinking, Constant Rumination And Unhealthy Behaviour Patterns So Prevalent In Depression

Many who feel better after two months of holistic therapy, still suffer from a constant barrage of negative thoughts and ruminations. These can be quite distressing. You may also find yourself regularly slipping into negative behaviour patterns, which contribute to your mood dropping. It is vital that we tackle these two issues if you hope to get better and stay well. Let's start with your thinking.

### Dealing With Negative Thinking/Rumination

This is one of the biggest obstacles on the journey from depression back to mental health. Countless books have been written on the subject, but the approaches presented in these books rarely work. The reason is that the emotional brain is so strong that it swamps the logical brain's ability to switch off or rationalise these ruminations.

There are three common pitfalls that most people fall into:

- They try to stop the negative ruminations swirling around their emotional brain – often by trying to distract themselves or by drinking alcohol.
- They assume that just because these thoughts are emanating from their mind, they must be true. We call this 'believing our own bullshit'!
- They believe that these thoughts are completely unique to them!

None of these beliefs are in fact true; it's just that we believe them to be so! Let's examine some typical thoughts emanating from the emotional brain in depression:

- 'I am a completely worthless person.'
- 'I have no intrinsic value to myself or others.'
- 'I am the invisible – or 'nothing' – man.'
- 'The world would not notice if I was not here.'
- 'I am just a burden on myself and others.'
- 'I am better avoiding social situations, as they will see me as I really am.'
- 'What is the point in going on?'
- 'My mood feels better, but why do I not feel that I am getting better?'
- 'I just can't see any future for myself or for those I love.'
- 'It all seems so bleak and dark in my world.'
- 'I am a weak person: only weak people get depressed.'
- 'I am so depressed about being depressed.'

These are only a handful of the unending stream of negative thoughts flowing through the mind of the person with depression. This may be the case even after two months of treatment, when the person is feeling better both in terms of their mood and physically. So clearly there is work to be done here. Although all forms of talk therapy can be used in this situation, I feel that this is where CBT comes into its own.

There are some golden rules in dealing with rumination and negative thinking:

- It is a complete waste of time trying to stop the flow of negative thoughts swishing through our emotional mind in depression. It is like going down to the sea, putting up your hand and trying to stop the tide!

- We have to become mindfully aware of these thoughts and, most importantly, accept their presence. Think of them as being like an 'unwelcome friend'!
- We have to see them for what they are: unhelpful, irrational thoughts created in our emotional brain by depression itself.
- We have to learn to observe them in a slightly detached manner, as we would clouds in the sky.
- We have to challenge the validity of the thoughts as being true. In other words, 'have I any proof that they are not complete bullshit?'
- If we start to view them with a sense of humour, it will go a long way towards diminishing their power in our minds.

The key, as suggested by the great CBT therapist Albert Ellis, is to analyse such negative thoughts created by the emotional brain and to see 'what is the overwhelming core of unhelpful beliefs beneath'? This was to be the classical CBT solution to what up to then seemed like a difficult problem to resolve.

Ellis's major insight related to the concept of self-worth. For behind almost every negative rumination created in the mind of the person with depression is the constant belief that they are of no value or worth.

Many focused on trying to challenge this unhelpful belief and help the person build up their sense of self-worth. Ellis decided, however, to throw away the whole measuring tool for assessing self-worth. He created the idea of accepting ourselves without condition!

Dealing with the unhelpful, unhealthy behaviour patterns in depression has challenged therapists and patients alike through the decades. Once again, CBT and other forms of behaviour therapy come into their own.

The real problem with our behaviour in depression is apathy. This is in turn fed by the negative ruminations already discussed. So even after two months of therapy, we may still be struggling to introduce the behavioural changes necessary to assist us in getting better and staying well.

# Depression

The commonest negative behavioural pattern is to avoid situations. If this won't work, the next pattern is to introduce safety behaviours to reduce the potential pitfalls our emotional brain is throwing up.

Let's examine a few common behaviour patterns and the thinking behind them. We include the consequences of such negative behaviours:

*'I won't exercise, as I am too tired, and what's the point anyway?'*
This of course isolates me further, and I miss the positive effects of exercise on my mood.

*'I will avoid social situations. I do this for a number of reasons: fatigue, apathy, and the knowledge that my presence will be a "downer" on the rest of the group. Who would want me as a dinner party guest?'*
This of course isolates me further and consolidates my belief that I am of little worth.

*'I will avoid taking on any new tasks, as I will get increasingly fatigued and end up more depressed.'*
This is a common false belief and of course ends up with the person believing that they are incapable of carrying out new tasks – which causes further drops in their mood and self-esteem.

*'I will use alcohol to lift my mood if I have to attend a particular party or event.'*
This of course worsens mood and makes me want to avoid subsequent parties. The reason for the drop in mood is of course alcohol, not the party!

*'I will avoid telling my partner, my family and my friends about my depression. If I do tell them, they will rate me even lower than I rate myself and my mood will drop further.'*
This is of course the opposite of what I should be doing. The more support one has, when depressed, from loved ones and friends, the quicker one will make a full recovery – and vice versa!

*'I avoid telling anyone at work. What would they think if they heard I was suffering from depression?'*

Once again, on occasion (with a very backward-looking employer, for instance) this might end up being the case. But in my experience, most employers are extremely sensitive to just how miserable one can feel when depressed. They may do the opposite of what your emotional mind suggests and actually try and be of some practical assistance!

*'I am going to stop taking my antidepressants, as I am embarrassed to admit taking them – even though I do admit to feeling better since starting the course.'*

As already discussed, this is going to lead to a relapse in your depression.

*'I will eat poorly, drink more alcohol and smoke more. These are the only things giving me any pleasure in my life at present.'*

Once again, this is using these substances as a coping mechanism to try and numb out how one is feeling. They will, of course, make us feel worse!

This is only a tiny segment of possible negative behaviours that people with depression may engage in. They are driven to these behaviours by a combination of fatigue (and fear of getting more fatigued), apathy, reduced enjoyment of the good things in life, and the relentless negative self-rating already discussed. To get better, we must recognise these negative behavioural patterns and gradually restructure our lives in a more positive manner. Once again, CBT is extremely useful in assisting us in this process. As we will see later, we use a simple 'ABC' method for this purpose. Suffice to say at this juncture that the secret is, firstly, to identify those behavioural patterns when depressed and to learn skills to challenge and restructure them in a more positive manner.

So in the examples given above, we might encourage the person to challenge their behaviour in relation to alcohol, exercise, nutrition and opening up to loved ones and work colleagues about our depression.

If we suffer from significant bouts of anxiety in between bouts of depression, or are carrying around major negative emotions like shame, guilt or hurt, how can we use the various forms of talk therapy, like CBT, to help us deal with them.

We have now dealt with stress triggers in our present lives, significant traumas in our past, and the constant negative ruminations that make the life of the person with depression so difficult. For the majority of people, this will cover most of the difficulties preventing them from getting better from depression.

There are, however, some other important emotions that can get in the way of a person making a full recovery. The commonest and most important is anxiety. But other people may be really struggling with emotions like hurt, shame and guilt. These may have been the 'mental stress triggers' which led them into depression to start with. If these relate to you, then please at least scan this section. If these emotions remain untreated, they will act as a constant magnet for depression now and in the future. If none of these emotions relate to you, then skip this section and move on. For the rest – read on!

## Anxiety

This is a major cause of distress and emotional turmoil for many. It is also innate to the human condition. All of us experience periods of acute and chronic anxiety, usually caused by specific events (e.g. exams or interviews) in the case of the former, or periods of financial difficulties in the latter. For a substantial number of people, anxiety develops a life of its own, seriously interfering with normal activities. For them, it moves from healthy to unhealthy anxiety. For some people, this will take the form of acute anxiety, as in panic attacks or phobias.

But from the point of view of depression, the commonest culprit is a form of chronic anxiety called general anxiety disorder (GAD), where the person presents with the following symptoms:

*   persistent feelings of intense anxiety and foreboding;
*   excessive worry about their health, family or job;
*   a constant sense of impending disaster.

This is often combined with the following physical or psychological symptoms, many of which are more distressing than the above:

- mental and physical fatigue, in some cases very severe
- poor concentration
- mind going blank in common social and domestic situations
- difficulties with memory
- muscle tension
- restlessness, tremor
- sleep difficulties (in up to 70 percent of sufferers), often associated with nightmares and teeth-grinding
- indecisiveness
- hypervigilance at all times
- regularly avoiding situations in everyday life due to fatigue and worrying about ability to cope
- never wanting to begin a new task, worrying that they will not have the energy to finish it, and thus becoming apathetic about such ventures, limiting the richness of their lives
- irritable bowel type symptoms like abdominal pain and loose bowel motions

The sufferer may also suffer bouts of acute anxiety – panicky-type episodes, with the following types of physical symptoms:

- tension headaches
- constant sighing
- palpitations
- stomach cramps and disturbance
- loss of appetite, with associated weight loss

Let's assume that you can relate to the anxiety/depression cycle. When you were in the throes of depression, some of your anxiety symptoms were engulfed by your low mood. After two months of therapy, you are feeling much better. You are, however, starting to feel some of the typical anxiety symptoms returning – particularly the constant negative worrying and ruminations. You are attending Dr Bill and he decides that you are now ready to tackle the problem.

You give him the example of hearing from a friend that a close associate had just been let go as a result of the recession. Following this telephone conversation, you began to feel incredibly anxious.

'And what was it about this news that bothered you?' he asks. You explain that you began to worry that you would be let go.

On further probing, you elaborate that if this happened, you and your partner would struggle to pay your mortgage, might have to let the house go, and could visualise yourselves on the street!

'So what demand did you make, in relation to this news?' he asked. You might reply that you must not lose your job, for all the above reasons.

'And what would it say about yourself, if you did lose your job?' he inquired. You replied that you would feel a complete failure, and very bad about yourself.

'So what did you do, when you started to become very anxious?' he asks. You admit ringing a work colleague for reassurance, checking out insurance cover on your house, drinking wine to calm yourself down, throwing your dinner away, and only being able to sleep after hours of replaying numerous scenarios as to what would happen if you were actually let go – trying to change the tape!

Dr Bill then explains the 'ABC' system, and puts the information gathered into the following format:

A: Activating Event:
- Trigger: The news that an associate had lost his job.
- Inference/Danger: That you would lose your job, would be unable to pay the mortgage, would lose the family home, and would end up homeless.

B: Belief/Demand: 'You must not lose your job, and if you did, would regard yourself as a failure.'

C: Consequences:
- Emotion: Anxiety
- Physical reactions: Stomach in knots, tension headache, palpitations, difficulties sleeping, difficulties breathing, and extreme fatigue.
- Behaviour: Rings work colleague, checks mortgage insurance, stops eating, misuses alcohol, has difficulty eating and sleeping.

Dr Bill would initially challenge your behaviour and would then challenge your unhealthy belief/demands, which we call the 'big MACS', and how they were contributing to your anxiety.

### 'M' STANDS FOR 'MUST'

People who suffer from anxiety live in the 'land of must!' where they use absolute terms like ought to, have to, should, must and so on, in relation to much of what happens to them in their lives. So he would challenge your need for 100 percent certainty that you would never lose your job. Was this possible in any aspect of life?

### 'A' STANDS FOR 'AWFUL'

Many, who suffer from anxiety, imagine the worst case scenario, where everything becomes a 'catastrophe'. So he would challenge your assumption that the worst would inevitably happen and that you are certain to lose your job, when there was absolutely no clear evidence to back this up. What would you do, if you actually lost it?

### 'C' STANDS FOR 'CAN'T STAND IT'

This is quite common in those who suffer from anxiety. He would challenge your view that you would not be able to cope if this actually happened.

### 'S' STANDS FOR 'SELF/OTHER RATING'

This lies at the heart of anxiety and indeed depression. This is where we not only judge ourselves but accept others' opinions of us as well. So he would challenge the concept that if you lost your job, that would make you a failure.

What he would actually be doing is getting you to see that when we suffer from persistent general anxiety which is causing us distress, we are usually:

- making impossible demands on ourselves
- catastrophising about the worst-case scenario without any proof to back it up

- assuming we will not be able to cope if we can't achieve these demands
- and finally, rating ourselves as being worthless if we can't achieve the un-achievable demands we have placed on ourselves.

You can immediately see the real connection between the way we deal with the negative rumination/belief that 'we are worthless' when depressed, and the tendency to do the same if we can't achieve these impossible demands when extremely anxious.

It is quite difficult to do this work on your own, and I recommend that you find a CBT therapist to assist you if you are suffering from the type of anxiety outlined above. If you can learn to stop trying to control life, cease rating your-self, you are on the road to really 'getting better' in relation to both anxiety and depression.

HURT is a powerful negative human emotion that can destroy the lives of those who harbour it, and frequently those close to them. I have often found it lurking in the background of those suffering from recurrent depression. Often the person might have gone as far as Step Three. They have accepted that they have depression and have come for assistance. They may have done well and, after two months, are feeling much better physically and mood-wise. But they are suffering from constant negative ruminations, and underneath these lies the hurt.

Many who have been hurt harbour deep-seated resentments about the way they were treated at various stages of their lives. Often the origin may lie in their upbringing. We discussed earlier the idea of the invalidating environ-ment, and this can be a powerful breeding ground for hurt.

At the core of hurt is the CBT concept that we are 'demanding to be treated fairly'. The problem is that the source of the hurt may lie in the past, and it may be difficult to resolve the original issue. For example, if I was sexually abused and tried to inform my parents but was ignored and shunned for even bringing up the subject, then my hurt may not be related to the actual abuse but to the fact that I was not listened to and was therefore treated unfairly. But there are many other examples, such as feeling that one was treated unfairly by siblings, in the workplace or within a sexual relationship.

People who have been hurt are often extremely brittle emotionally and tend to lash out at anyone they feel is treating them unfairly, even if this is not the case. They carry and nurse the hurt – which becomes an integral part of who they are. The problem is that deep down they rate themselves as failures for allowing the hurt to have occurred at all. It is not a big step from there to the sense of complete worthlessness so key to depression. If you can identify this emotion in yourself, then it is vital that you seek out help. You will not be able to handle this emotion on your own: it is like dealing with gunpowder – extremely explosive. You will need to work with a talk therapist to locate the source of your hurt. If you are still finding it difficult to let it go, then CBT is again very useful. In general terms, the CBT therapist would help you challenge your unhealthy demand to be treated fairly and also the negative behaviour which is making you lash out at so many who may try to help. It is beyond the scope of this book to deal with it any further.

If you do suffer from hurt and are brave enough to deal with it, then you are on the road to getting better, long term, from your depression. If not, it will be a struggle!

SHAME is another powerful human emotion and one that is driving some in modern Ireland to suicide. We all, as human beings, rate ourselves and are extremely vulnerable to allowing other people to do the same. If life throws issues at us that trigger this vulnerability, then our instinctive tendency is to hide it from others.

There are numerous examples of this in practice. If I have lost my job, I may be ashamed of my neighbours finding out that I am now on the dole. I may feel ashamed that they will discover my secret, judge me and find me wanting. So my behaviour may be to leave my house every day, only returning in the evening, as if all is well. This is happening in many estates throughout the country. For others, similar issues with housing and debt are a source of shame.

Others may be ashamed that their sexuality may be exposed. Many gay people live lives of shame and fear that their secret life will be exposed to family, friends or community. Some will become depressed with this powerful negative emotional stress trigger. Some will even take their own lives if their secret is going to be exposed. Also at risk can be those who are afraid that an illicit relationship might be exposed to the scrutiny of their family or community.

For others, it might be that they were raped, abused or had an abortion. They may be ashamed of what happened to them and what others would think of them if their secret was revealed – to loved ones or the community in general. Some people will even become ashamed of the fact that they have depression. This can lead to a vicious circle of depression leading to shame, leading to a further deterioration of depression.

If you are reading this and can relate to this emotion, it is important to seek assistance. If you are suffering from resulting bouts of depression, then it is essential to deal with shame. Once again, CBT can be of assistance in achieving this goal.

At the core of shame is the unhealthy belief that 'I must accept other people's opinion of me'. Once again I particularly appeal to those who are having problems with sexual identity to come for assistance. Engage with talk therapists who are comfortable in dealing with unhelpful emotions (of which shame is one) associated with this area. If you are having the twin problems of shame and depression, your life will be truly miserable unless you seek out counselling or therapy to deal with your concerns.

Shame, on its own or linked with depression, can be a powerful suicide trigger. If it is an issue for you, come for help!

GUILT is another important emotion linked with depression. We are all remorseful about events that happen in our lives. But when remorse turns to the more unhealthy emotion of guilt, it can destroy us if left to fester.

I have often come across guilt in the background to depression. It exhausts the person's emotional resilience and some who are prone to this illness may succumb. The commonest reasons for guilt are usually related to abortions or illicit relationships with either men or women. For others, it may be the way they treated parents, siblings or children at key periods in their lives. At the heart of guilt is the demand that 'we should have known what to do and should have been able to do it.' All those who are suffering from guilt want to rewrite the tape and change whatever decisions they made, which they now feel are wrong.

Many of those who feel guilty over such situations may find themselves again in a vicious circle of guilt, leading to depression, leading back to guilt, and so on. If you are reading this and can identify with this emotion and this cycle, then, again, I recommend that you admit this emotion to yourself and engage with talk therapy to deal with it. CBT can be useful as an adjunct if, despite counselling, you can't move beyond this emotion. The therapist will help you look again at, and challenge, your demand to change your decision and behaviour.

## Let's Summarise Step Three

We must continue the holistic approach involving lifestyle changes and drug therapy, if relevant, started in Step Two.

We must analyse the major stress triggers which may have led to the arrival of this particular bout of depression in our life.

We must examine the possibility of counselling or therapy if there are issues in relation to grief, abuse, significant difficulties in our past, addiction, major traumas, and so on.

We must learn new skills to help deal with the negative thinking, constant rumination and unhealthy behaviour patterns so prevalent in depression.

In general the first, second and fourth sections apply to almost every person with depression and are relevant to every bout they may encounter. The third section is only relevant to those who have experienced the particular difficulties detailed. If they do not relate to you – move on.

Now let's revisit some of those whom we met earlier and assess how they put these points into practice.

## Gerry's Story (revisited)

We met Gerry in an earlier chapter. Here we will summarise the main details of his story to date. He was a twenty-two-year-old college student whose parents were high achievers and who were anxious that Gerry would do well at college. He had grown up in an environment where his own feelings and emotions were never validated, and this led to him becoming his own greatest critic.

His father was also intolerant to conditions like anxiety, stress, and particularly depression. To him, these demonstrated that the individuals in question were weaklings, and to be avoided. Gerry unconsciously absorbed these emotional messages and became trapped in his own world of depression.

As we saw earlier, Gerry suffered significant depression in his first two years in college but things came to a head in his third year when he decided to take his own life. His life was only saved by a call to a college helpline. This was followed by him attending a self-help group, meeting Jane a fellow sufferer with depression, who encourages him to attend a college counsellor and Dr Bill who had helped her through her own difficulties. By the time Gerry sees Dr Bill he has achieved his first step on the journey to recovery. He has come to accept that he was depressed and needs some assistance. He has also chosen his guide.

He attended Dr Bill with Jane, and found him very empathetic. He revealed his difficulties during the previous three years and, on deeper probing, the hurt he had been carrying in relation to his father.

Dr Bill explains that they will return to the latter at a later stage. Firstly, they have to move on to Step Two: helping Gerry to feel better. He lays out a holistic programme involving exercise, nutrition, supplements, and not taking alcohol for the foreseeable future, until his mood improves. They discuss the ins and outs of drug therapy and, on Dr Bill's recommendation, Gerry begins a course of modern antidepressants. They also agree that it would be helpful to continue attending the depression self-help group. Gerry, on his advice, also decides to start using a dawn simulator, as the winter months had always been more difficult for him mood-wise. They also discuss safety measures if thoughts of self-harm increased at any stage.

On initially reviewing stress triggers in Gerry's life, Dr Bill recommends that he should take a period of eight weeks off college. They liaise with the college, who are happy to assist him during this process. They agree that if he falls too far behind in his studies, his year can be deferred on medical grounds. Within six to eight weeks, Gerry is feeling much better. His mood is up, suicide thoughts have receded, and energy, concentration and drive have improved. He is exercising daily, although finding this difficult, and his nutrition has greatly improved.

But the constant negative rumination thoughts that he was worthless continued, and the deeper-seated hurt remained lurking in his subconscious. But now Dr Bill felt that he was physically and psychologically ready to move to Step Three, where Dr Bill would assist him, through talk therapy, in dealing with some of these issues. He firstly encourages Gerry to continue the holistic therapy approach that had helped him to feel better particularly to continue his drug therapy. Gerry, like every person with depression, wondered if he could cease it now that he was feeling better. They also review his main stress trigger: the final year of his college course. Gerry at this stage feels that his concentration and energy have improved to a point where he feels capable of returning to his studies. They decide that he will give it a trial. If it becomes too difficult, they will revisit the matter.

Now Dr Bill assists him in the area of negative thinking. He asks Gerry to give him a recent example of a particular negative thought coming to the fore. Gerry details meeting a friend from college, with whom he shared the information that he had taken a short break from his studies due to depression. His friend sympathised, but when Gerry came home, the thoughts began:

- 'I am so weak that I had to take time off studying. Why can't I be like everybody else and simply get on with things?'
- 'I felt so embarrassed to admit that I was suffering from depression. I know that it is only an illness, but I still feel so depressed about being depressed!'
- 'I could see in my friend's face that he pitied me. I can understand how he would feel like that, for am I not completely worthless anyway?'
- 'I know my family feel that I am a weakling, but now even my friends will see me as I really am: weak, boring, useless, and much to be pitied!'
- 'It's always going to be like this!'
- 'I felt so bad meeting Tim. I have always liked him but will try and avoid meeting him again, as I ended up feeling so down afterwards.'
- 'In fact I will spend less time out on the campus, and more in my apartment. At least there I feel safer and will not have to keep meeting people who only confirm what I already know: I am crap!'

Dr Bill uses this example to help Gerry understand what is going on in his emotional mind. He explains about the power of the emotional mind over the logical mind, and how we end up believing these thoughts to be true! He explains the 'ABC' system to Gerry, and together they do an 'ABC' on the above example.

A: Activating Event:
- Trigger: Meeting his friend and discussing his break from studies as a result of depression.
- Inference/Danger: That as a result of depression, he is a weak person, and not able to study in the normal way. That he is much to be pitied: only a weak, worthless person ends up getting depression. That all the criticisms levelled at him by his family in the past are true, and only confirm how worthless he truly is.

B: Belief/Demand:
- That because he has depression and has to take a break from his studies, he is a complete failure and of no worth.

C: Consequences:
- Emotion: Depression
- Physical Reactions: Fatigue, reduction in concentration, increased anxiety, loss of enjoyment of his meal that evening, and so on.
- Behaviour: Avoids meeting his friend again. He spends more time isolated in his apartment in case he might meet other friends. He also spends hours ruminating about the meeting, and struggles to sleep.

Dr Bill firstly challenged Gerry's behaviour. How would hiding himself away in his apartment and avoiding meeting friends assist him in his goal of getting better? They agreed that it was just avoidant behaviour and that it would be healthier for Gerry to do the opposite – namely to socialise more with his friends. Constantly ruminating on what had happened was not helping either. It was of course impossible to stop such ruminations, but it would be a good idea to take out a pen and paper and work out why the meeting with his friend had bothered him to start with.

He then explained that they could challenge his interpretation of what had happened. Could he prove that just because one got a bout of depression, one was weak and worthless? Would he do the same if the illness in question was diabetes? He noted that they would deal with his family situation later. The simplest way to deal with the problem was to challenge the belief that he was worthless and a complete failure – for it was this false belief that underpinned his negative ruminations about himself. He asked Gerry a good-humoured question (which is used by a leading CBT therapist friend and colleague, Brian Kelly): 'What does a worthless person look like?' He also asked: 'What does a failure look like?' Can you describe what the word "worth" actually means?'

Gerry, to his surprise, struggled to describe just what a worthless person looked like, and similarly could not really explain a number of other adjectives his emotional mind used to describe himself – like 'useless', 'hopeless', 'awful' and 'boring'. He realised that he had been using all these terms to describe himself. He had come to accept them as completely accurate as a way of portraying himself in his emotional mind. Dr Bill explained that it was our internal pathological critic which was generating this 'bullshit'. The problem, he explained, is that when we start to believe it is true, we get into difficulties. In depression, he explained, our emotional brain goes into this negative mode and our logical brain gets sidelined. The key is to use the latter to challenge the former.

If Gerry could do away with the whole idea of worth to start with, then he would learn to accept himself without conditions. So whether or not he suffered from bouts of depression, or indeed any other illness, he would not rate himself or accept other people's rating of him. He would be free to be 'just himself'.

Gerry could now see that this was indeed the shortcut to getting better. Never again would he accept that the term 'worthless', for example, meant that he was just that. He was now free, for the first time in his life, to accept himself as he was, and not all the time to wish that he was somebody else with that imaginary person always being perfect!

Over the next few months, Gerry works with Dr Bill, doing plenty of 'ABC' homework to challenge his negative thinking, and soon found these ruminations decreasing and, more importantly, becoming of much less significance in his life. He was on his way to becoming better.

However, one final hurdle remained. For Gerry still had difficulties with his family, and deep-seated resentments remained. He was still very hurt in relation to his father, who had never validated him and who had been less than sympathetic about his bout of depression – which he considered further proof that his son was indeed a weakling!

To deal with this initially, Dr Bill sent Gerry to a therapist to explore many of the issues relating to his childhood and upbringing. While Gerry found this extremely helpful, he was unable to move beyond the block of hurt. This was the last remaining obstacle to him getting better.

Once again, Dr Bill decides to do an 'ABC' as he feels that Gerry is now ready to deal with this thorny issue. Once again, he looks for an example of something which had occurred between his father and himself that triggered the emotion strongly. Gerry gave the example of coming home to explain to his parents that he was taking eight weeks off studying as he was experiencing a bout of depression. They do an 'ABC' of the event; it went like this:

A: Activating Event
- Trigger: Informing his father that he has depression and would have to take eight weeks off studying.
- Inference/danger: His father was not really interested in any 'excuse' that he was suffering from an illness like depression, as he regarded this as a weakness. If he was a 'real man', like some of his brothers, he would be 'getting on with it' and would stop feeling 'sorry for himself'! He felt that, once again, his voice was not being heard by his father, who rated his siblings as being much 'stronger' and of much greater value to him.

B: Belief/Demand
- That he must be treated fairly by his father. If not, he, Gerry, was a failure.

C: Consequences
- Emotion: Hurt and depression

- Physical reactions: The usual symptoms of depression
- Behaviour: Gerry tried to avoid any contact with his family, especially his father, ruminated constantly on how unfair it was to be treated in this way, and found himself lashing out at siblings and even close friends if he felt they were taking him for granted and, in his eyes, not treating him fairly.

Dr Bill explained that hurt was one of the most difficult of all human emotions both to experience and to deal with, and that it often occurred as a result of being reared in an environment where we were not validated i.e. nobody accepted our emotions as having any place. If we were constantly overlooked and criticised, we began to carry on our backs the huge weight of hurt.

Once again, he challenged Gerry's behaviour. Was avoiding his family, while completely understandable, actually helping Gerry in any way? Was constant rumination, or fighting with family members or close friends, helping him deal with his hurt, and was he just 'numbing' the emotion by lashing out at others.

Was it not better to try and deal with the hurt itself?

He then moved on to examine Gerry's thinking in relation to this particular event. They agree that Dr Bill could challenge his interpretation that just because his father held such views on depression, for example, that Gerry had to accept those views as being true!

But the real key was to examine Gerry's demand that 'he must be treated fairly'. This may seem like a reasonable statement. In practice, it was an absolute demand, rather than a preference – which would be much healthier. Was there any law in the universe that stated that his father, or indeed anybody else, 'must' treat him fairly?

Was Gerry carrying the load of hurt on his back in relation to his father actually helping him in his life? Was it not better to consider dropping the hurt – not because it would help his father, but rather because it would help Gerry himself?

In both cases, they were free to rate behaviour but not themselves. If Gerry accepted this, then he was free to forgive his father but was still allowed to tackle him in relation to his inappropriate behaviour.

As a result of this session, Gerry made a great breakthrough, deciding that this hurt had done enough damage in his life. He ends up dropping the hurt and forgiving his dad – but not before going home and having a serious conversation with him in relation to his behaviour.

It was to be a watershed moment for both him and his parents. His father was forced for the first time to review his own behaviour. He was quite shaken when Gerry revealed how close he had come to dying by suicide. Suddenly he began to see the consequences of his actions and vowed to make concerted efforts to change. The warm embrace between them at the end of this conversation was the beginning of a new relationship which would end up nourishing both of them.

After nine months, Gerry had travelled vast distances on the journey back to getting well from his depression. He had faithfully persisted with the holistic therapy programme outlined. The work done with Dr Bill and others had transformed his life and would bear much fruit in the years to come. Later we will see how he managed, not only to get better, but to stay well!

## Peter's Story (revisisted)

We met Peter earlier. Here we will summarise his story to date. He is a man in his late thirties who has had one prior bout of depression, while at college. He had a good job in a company which boomed during the Celtic Tiger era. Like so many in modern Ireland, he fell into the trap of taking out a high mortgage, together with his partner Marie. They had two children, Nessa and John. The company he worked for went into liquidation and Peter only received minimum redundancy. He experiences a bout of major depression and is filled with shame and guilt. He is unable to look after his family 'like a real man would'. He becomes hopeless and despairing and plans to take his own life, considering making it look like an accident, so that his family can claim some life insurance.

Thankfully, as we saw earlier, the intervention of his little daughter saved him and he ended up coming to see Dr Bill. He has already been working with him on the second step of the journey back to mental health. He has completed the first eight weeks of his holistic therapy of exercise, nutrition, supplements, drug therapy, and ceasing alcohol, and is feeling much better in relation to his mood and physical symptoms. He is now ready to begin Step Three.

Dr Bill encourages him to continue the holistic package that had helped him feel so much better. He then turned his attention to the stress triggers that had set off this particular bout of depression. The big issue was of course financial in nature. There was also concern that as a result of their high mortgage and the loss of his job, he and Marie could end up losing their home.

The first thing Peter had to realise was that it was the 'situation that was abnormal, not him'. So it is this they had to address now. He advised Peter to attend a financial advisor and to lay out his difficulties with his bank. He ends up doing both. As a result, his loans are put together in one long-term loan with the credit union and the bank assists him in restructuring his mortgage. He now involves his wife Marie in all decisions and feels better that they are handling the situation together.

The other big stress is, of course, work. Now that he is feeling better, Peter realises that he is going to need retraining, and contacts the relevant training bodies. He also considers the possibility of starting his own business. As Dr Bill had explained, the more active he became, rather than constantly ruminating on all that had happened, the better he would feel.

Once he had dealt with these issues, Dr Bill turned to Peter's negative thoughts. As he had with Gerry, he helped Peter come to terms with these ruminations. This resulted in a major lift in his mood. For the first time in his life, he began to accept himself.

Peter was now ready to deal with the other two emotions that had nearly led to his demise – namely shame and guilt. They started with shame. Dr Bill asked him to revisit the feelings of shame that had led him to consider ending it all. What was the trigger?

Peter explained that it was the loss of his job and income that that had triggered this emotion. Dr Bill explained the 'ABC' method to him, and together they did an 'ABC' on this trigger.

A:  Activating Event
- Trigger: Loss of job combined with sudden drop in income.

- Inference/Danger: As a result, he would be unable to support his family and would lose their home. Those who loved him, and those in the wider family and community, would learn of his inability to be a 'good provider' and judge him to be a failure.

B: Belief/Demand
- He must accept their opinion – that he is a failure.

C: Consequences
- Emotion: Shame and depression
- Physical reactions: The usual symptoms of depression
- Behaviour: Initially, he tried to hide his predicament from his wife and family. He ruminated constantly on how he would cope if his difficulties became more widely known. He also ended up drinking and isolating himself from others. He avoided opening up letters from financial institutions so that he would not have to deal with the issue.

Dr Bill firstly challenges whether these behaviours had made matters better or worse. They agree that it had been the latter. So Peter agrees openly to discuss issues with those closest to him and to stop isolating himself. He also continued to avoid alcohol, as already advised.

But it is Peter's thinking that Dr Bill really challenges. The irrational belief that he 'must accept the judgement of others' is the real core of the problem. Once we hand over power to other people to 'judge us', we are always going to end up in difficulty.

For example, how could losing his job in the middle of the greatest economic disaster since the 1930s turn him into a failure? And why should other people be given the dubious honour of rating us just because we are unfortunate victims of such a recession? We can only do our best each day. After that, we must leave the rest to fate. When Peter grasps the power of the allegory, he feels a huge weight lifting off his shoulders. Suddenly he truly grasps that it was the situation that was abnormal, not himself. Never again would he accept other people's rating of him.

Once the penny dropped, the shame was gone and Peter was free to get better. But one obstacle remained: guilt over his decision to take out the massive mortgage to begin with.

To deal with this, Dr Bill looks for an example of this in practice. Peter talks about a day before he initially came to see Dr Bill when he received a letter from the bank which he refused to open. Once again, they do an 'ABC' on this trigger:

A:  Activating Event
- Trigger: The arrival of a letter from the bank
- Inference/Danger: The bank was going to pull the plug on their mortgage and they might lose everything. He had made so many bad decisions that had led to this crisis. 'How could he have been so stupid?'

B:  Belief/Demand
- That 'he should have known better than to take out a high mortgage and should not have done it'. He also feels that because he made the wrong decision, he is a failure.

C:  Consequences
- Emotion: Guilt and depression
- Physical reactions: The usual symptoms of depression
- Behaviour: He tried to hide his predicament from his wife and family. He ended up ruminating constantly about how stupid he was for taking out such a mortgage. He avoided opening letters from the bank, as they only reinforced his feelings of guilt and stupidity.

Once again, they agree that his behaviour was not helping the situation. But the real key lay in his demand 'that he should have known what to do and should not have done it'. Dr Bill then asks him if he has the 'sight'. Peter reassures him that he definitely had not, or else he would have won the Lotto long ago! But Dr Bill then challenges him: 'If you don't have the sight, then how could you have known that the world economy and banking sectors were to collapse, and that you would lose your job?'

He went on to explain that when people are guilty, they always want to change a decision made at a particular time in their lives, and usually within a definite set of circumstances. All of us make decisions on a daily basis – sometimes right and sometimes wrong. But we make them with the information available at the time and in the emotional state we happen to be in. Unless we have the power to see into the future, we cannot predict at the time of making a decision whether it will work out or not. We have to let ourselves off the hook if we have done the best we could at the time with the information available and it doesn't work out as expected.

Peter has now learned to deal not only with negative rumination thoughts but also with emotions like shame and guilt. He has made the last step in his journey to get well. Later we will see how things worked out.

## Kate's Story (revisited)

Earlier in the book, we also met Kate, who is twenty-five. Here we will summarise her story to date. You may remember that, despite coming from an extremely abusive family situation where she had been physically and sexually abused by her alcoholic father, she found herself in a relationship with an abusive partner. She had a three-year-old child and desperately relied on her partner to help rear him. She started off with panic attacks, secondary to being anxious (due to the abuse she had received), and then became severely depressed. She was getting serious suicide thoughts that she and her baby might be better off if they were no longer around. Life intervenes however and she ends up in A&E following a broken jaw secondary to another assault. There she meets a social worker who passes her on to see Dr Bill. Her journey has begun.

By the time she reaches him, her mood is extremely low. Her child is now in temporary foster care. At least she is in a place of safety where her abusive partner cannot now assault her. Dr Bill is extremely concerned for her safety but heartened by the fact that she is ready to accept help for the sake of her child. They agree a safety protocol and she sees him regularly until she is feeling better.

He institutes a holistic package of exercise, nutrition, supplements and avoiding alcohol. He starts her on an antidepressant, to be prescribed weekly until her suicidal thoughts subside. He also encourages her to separate completely from her abusive partner.

For Kate the next six weeks are a real battle, but slowly her mood lifts and her appetite, sleep, energy and concentration improve. The suicide thoughts, which had reached the planning stage, now start to subside. She seeks, and is granted, a protection order and presses charges against her abusive partner. She is also able to see her child for short periods, under supervision. After eight weeks she is feeling much better and is ready to face the serious challenges in her battle to become well again.

Dr Bill encourages her to stay on the regimen as detailed. He also advises her to remain in the hostel until suitable alternative accommodation can be found. Now it is time for Kate to come to terms with her difficulties, through talk therapy.

Her immediate stress triggers are the loss of her child and the fear that her former partner will find her and seriously assault her. Dr Bill encourages her to continue down the legal route in relation to her former partner and to work with her social worker in relation to her child.

He then turns his attention to her negative thinking. Kate still felt that she was worthless and not worth saving. It was only her child that kept her going.

The years of abuse at the hands of her alcoholic father and then her partner had left their mark. She felt that she 'deserved to be treated in such a manner'. Dr Bill felt that she needed counselling and referred her to a therapist specialising in sexual abuse. She grasped the idea like a drowning woman grasping a lifebuoy; it would eventually bring her to safety.

By eight months, Kate is thriving and has her son back. With the help of her social worker she moves into a new flat; her former partner has ceased to be a problem. She finds the sessions with her therapist in relation to her abuse extremely difficult and often ends up distressed and in tears. But bit by bit she is learning new ways of coping with her past.

However, there is still one important area she continues to struggle with. This is the hurt and anger she is carrying, not towards her father but towards her mother, who had failed to protect her. As a result of her therapy, she was able to deal with the anger she felt towards her father, but not the hurt towards her mother. She returns to Dr Bill seeking help.

Dr Bill is delighted with her overall progress. Her mood has returned to normal and suicide thoughts have become a thing of the past. She has put on weight and is happily bonding with her child. She had worked hard with her therapist, but Dr Bill knew that if she persisted in carrying this hurt, it would return in the future, to cause her difficulties.

He asks Kate to give him an example of when she had felt this emotion in relation to her mother. Kate answered that on a recent visit she had admitted to undergoing therapy to deal with her abuse. Her mother had become upset and tried to deny what had happened. 'Kate was only thinking like this because she was depressed.' 'Your father was a difficult man and he had a problem with alcohol but would never behave in the way you are describing!'

Kate described coming away in tears, feeling very hurt, and for the following few days her mood dropped. Thankfully she was still attending her therapist, who supported her during this crisis. Dr Bill felt that this was an excellent chance to assist Kate in dealing with her hurt. He explained the 'ABC' concept to her, and they do an 'ABC' on this meeting with her mother.

A: Activating Event
- Trigger: The visit to her mother, where the latter denied her father had abused Kate.
- Inference/Danger: That her mother did not believe her story. She was also choosing to put her dead husband's name above her own daughter's health and welfare. She obviously thought very little of her daughter to treat her in such a manner.

B: Belief/Demand
- That she, Kate, must be treated fairly by her mother; she was a failure for allowing her mother to treat her unfairly.

C: Consequences
- Emotion: Hurt and depression
- Physical reactions: The usual symptoms of depression

- Behaviour: She retreated back into herself and didn't emerge in public for two days. During that period she relived the conversation over and over, with intense emotional bursts of hurt followed by feeling depressed. 'How could I have let her treat me in such a way? I am really weak for allowing her to do so!' When her mother rang to see how she was, she shut down the conversation abruptly and vowed to avoid her as much as possible in order to prevent such a recurrence. She also began to question her own version of affairs. Was she really abused or was it all in her imagination? Maybe she had in some way behaved in such a manner as to attract her father's attention? The negative thoughts just buzzed around her head. She found it difficult not to rate herself after this encounter.

Dr Bill empathised with her over what had been a very difficult encounter. However, if Kate was going to get better, she had to find a way to get over this hurdle. He challenged her behaviour. Was it helping her in any way to try and avoid her mother, to isolate herself, or to try to deny that anything had ever happened? They agreed that none of this was assisting her in getting better.

He then challenged her absolute demand to be treated fairly. Have any of us the right to demand that others treat us the way we feel we should be treated? In practice, although we would all prefer to be treated as such, we cannot demand this, or we will end up suffering as a result. He also asked her whether carrying the hurt towards her mother was helping her in her life. Kate replied that it was not.

He gives her the following exercise. She has to fill a rucksack with stones and carry it on her back for the day. At the end of this, she has to write down how she felt when carrying it, and what it felt like when she removed it!

On her return, she admits that the exercise made the point! She was exhausted when carrying the load and felt much lighter when it was gone. 'That is what you want me to do with the hurt,' she says. 'But how can I drop it?'

Dr Bill then explains that it is her absolute demand that her mother should have treated her fairly in the past and the present that was the issue. 'If you forgive her, the person, while accepting that her behaviour is not appropriate, then you can let the load go. You do so not for your mother's sake but for your own!' Kate suddenly sees the light, and a huge load is lifted off her shoulders. Now, with Dr Bill's help, she begins to see her own mother as someone who was probably as much a victim of her father's behaviour as she was herself. It is the start of a real recovery from her depression. She now not only feels better but has actually travelled a long way down the road towards getting better. Does she stay well? We will see later.

## Christina's Story (revisited)

We also met Christina earlier in the book. She came from a family where depression was a significant illness affecting both her mum and dad. As you may remember, she was extremely traumatised by finding her mum almost dead following a major suicidal overdose of tablets.

She was now in her mid-thirties, and struggling. She was extremely bright, and managing to hold down her job as a teacher, albeit with some difficulty. Over the years, Christina had become socially isolated. She had a number of good relationships but would keep breaking them off, feeling that the men in question deserved better. Her world was narrowing down to a daily battle simply to get up, carry out her normal domestic chores and deal with her teaching post.

Following a period of significant stress at work, her mood plummets. She had had some bad experiences with modern antidepressants and had attended a multitude of doctors, therapists and the whole gamut of alternative practitioners. Luckily, on this occasion, her principal persuades her to attend Dr Bill and to take an extended break from work to get some help for her depression.

Christina comes to see Dr Bill detailing the many and varied therapies she has tried over the years. She also expressed her difficulties with the modern antidepressants she had been prescribed over the years and how hopeless she felt about ever feeling 'normal' again. He explains the holistic approach to her, and she is agreeable to the lifestyle changes suggested, but admits to struggling to find the energy to walk for half an hour. She also agrees to ceasing alcohol, on which she had become increasingly dependent.

Dr Bill then decides to try her on an old-fashioned antidepressant. She agrees to cease alternative therapies until she has seen how his approach might work. He sees her regularly over the next six to eight weeks and she remains off work during this period. To her surprise, her mood, sleep, energy and appetite all improve, and she feels better than she has done in years. But she is plagued with constant internal ruminations that she is worthless.

Dr Bill now feels that she is ready to move on to Step Three. He encourages her to continue her holistic package and stay off work until she has improved further. They examine the main stress issues. The two that come up are her perfectionism at work, no matter what it is costing her, and the buried trauma of living with the fear that her mother would take her own life. Christina admits that she has spent much of her childhood and early adult life living with the latter. She also admits to being constantly anxious and on high alert as a result. She has also felt that if she was a 'better' child her mother would not have been driven to such actions. To deal with both of these things, Dr Bill sends Christina to a therapist, who helps her explore this and come to terms with it. Meanwhile, he takes on her negative rumination thoughts.

He explains that these thoughts are normal in depression – 'a real, unwanted friend who will just not go away!' It is a complete waste of time to try and stop them. We need to learn to accept the thoughts but also to challenge their content. The typical thoughts that we are worthless, useless, and so on are especially common in those who suffer from repeated bouts of depression. The latter often have a very strong history of depression in their families.

Once again, as detailed earlier, Dr Bill challenges the whole concept of 'what a worthless person looks like.

Christina continues to improve over the next six months and works hard on her lifestyle changes and with her therapist. As is often the case, she hits a wall in relation to her struggle with the post-traumatic stress reaction experienced from finding her mother so close to death. Her therapist sends her back to Dr Bill to help her make a breakthrough.

He is delighted with her progress. She is now ready to deal with the buried trauma that may have triggered the depressions which she has been experiencing from an early age. He revisits the occurrence with her using the 'ABC' model, which he explains. They come up with the following:

# Depression

A:  Activating Event
- Trigger: Finding her mother unconscious following an overdose
- Inference/Danger: That her mother could have died. That in some way, if she had been a better child, she could have prevented her mother from trying to take her own life. She also lived from then on with the fear that it could happen again, or that her dad might do the same. It made her increasingly aware as the years passed of how vulnerable we all are and how something can happen which can take either ourselves or a loved one away.

B:  Belief / Demand
- That she must be completely certain that her mother, or indeed anyone close to her, will not die.

C:  Consequences
- Emotion: Anxiety and depression
- Physical Reactions: The usual symptoms of anxiety and depression
- Behaviour: She spent most of her childhood (and indeed the present) hovering over her mum and dad in case something terrible might happen – something that she could have prevented. When she gets older, she even begins to scan the environment for danger in relation to herself or others. This anxiety has spread into every part of her life – even work! When she is depressed, she gets relief, as she feels so awful that her anxiety fades into the background. But as she recovers, her anxiety recurs.

Dr Bill reassures her that this is a classical example of a buried trauma from the past lurking in our emotional brain triggering anxiety and depression. They agree that the years of 'hovering' over her mum and dad did nothing to assist the situation but instead contributed to Christina becoming increasingly anxious. He explained that it was normal following a near-death occurrence in those close to us to become overprotective. If we are going to deal with it, we have to change our behaviour and cease 'hovering and scanning our environment constantly for danger'.

The secret lay in our demand for 100 percent certainty that neither ourselves nor anyone close to us can experience a serious illness or trauma and die. He challenged Christina on the whole concept of certainty and the fact that it is impossible to achieve this in most parts of our lives. He helps her examine and dismantle her demands for control in other areas of life particularly in relation to issues at home and at school. Over a number of visits, Christina begins to realise that it was her constant demand for certainty, order, security and perfection which was causing her problems, and she learns, over time, to let go of this demand.

Gradually she comes to terms with her post-traumatic experiences and approaches the future in a much more relaxed and realistic manner.

She has completed the last chain in her journey towards getting better. We will see how she learns to stay well later!

These four cases show exactly how a combination of a holistic therapy package for the first eight weeks, followed by a genuine review of both present and past stress triggers, and learning how to deal with our negative ruminations and unhealthy emotions like hurt and guilt, can transform the lives of many.

But now let's examine the Holy Grail of depression: learning how to *stay well*.

# PART SIX

## Step Four (9 months onwards)
## How To Stay Well!

If you have 'walked the line' till now, we will assume that you are well physically and psychologically. We will now move on to the last phase. This involves disengaging from some of the therapies you have been using and building a solid platform from which you can look forward to the future, hopefully free from depression.

We have to put in an important caveat here. If any book, therapist or doctor claims to guarantee that you will never suffer a further bout of depression – beware! This is an impossible promise to deliver on. Major depression, by its very nature, is a recurrent illness, and one which can be extremely unpredictable. The best we can do is to try to reduce the risk of such a recurrence to an absolute minimum. We will be examining various approaches that have been shown to assist in this regard.

We will divide Step Four into two phases. The first is from nine months to one year, and the second is from one year onwards.

### From Nine Months To One Year

In this phase, the person with depression may feel vulnerable. They have worked hard both to feel better and to get better. Now they are back to themselves and ready to move on. But this brings its own anxieties! Many are terrified that they will become depressed again if they disengage from some of the therapies which helped them get better.

There are three important decisions to be made at this stage:

- Whether to continue with the major lifestyle changes outlined in the first three steps.
- If, when and how to disengage from drug therapy.
- If, when and how to disengage from talk therapy.

When we are feeling miserable, we are prepared to make significant changes in our life, but when we are back to ourselves, we become careless in relation to continuing with these changes. Depression is a classical example of this in action. All the evidence points to the fact that continuing with the lifestyle changes outlined earlier is crucial to staying well.

## Exercise

Exercise has been shown to help us not only to get better but to stay well. Earlier in the book, we detailed its positive effects on our brain and stress system. I encourage patients to try to build thirty minutes of exercise into their daily lives – for life! Over the years, I have been astonished by the number of people, presenting with a relapse of depression, who have dropped their daily exercise regimen. It seems like such an innocuous therapy that many fail to appreciate its effectiveness. So at nine months to one year, I encourage patients to keep up their daily thirty minutes of exercise, no matter what else they do.

## Nutrition

While often trotted out as the only way to stay well in relation to depression, nutrition is important, but not to the same degree as simple exercise. That said, it makes sense to continue a sensible diet of fish, fresh vegetables and fruit, and plenty of nuts and seeds.

## Supplements

Similarly, supplements are easy to take. I usually recommend a daily B complex and Omega 3 fish oils for life.

## Alcohol

This is one area where we need to be especially careful. Many are happy to avoid alcohol when they are feeling very down. Once they have made a full recovery, there is a risk that they may return to drinking more alcohol than is appropriate. Significant amounts of alcohol may bring our mood down, leading to a recurrence of depression. We must be honest with ourselves as to how much (if any) alcohol we can take without our mood dropping. Many people are caught out by the fact that, while they are drinking, they may feel less anxious and in a good mood, but over the following few days their mood may drop. If this happens, we have to acknowledge it and make the necessary changes.

## Managing Stress

This is another lifestyle change we need to keep assessing. While getting better from our bout of depression, we may have been careful to review stress in our life and make changes. But when we are well, we may return to old ways and expose ourselves to too much stress. I feel that we need to review this area at least once a week – and to be brutally honest in our assessments.

We also need to enlist the help of a partner, family member or close friend to keep an eye on us. If they notice us getting toxically stressed, we must accept their opinion and review the situation. It is sensible to keep an eye on potential troublesome areas like personal finances. If we sense trouble on the horizon, early intervention may protect us from further a relapse.

We should take proper holidays and make sure that we get plenty of rest. It is also important to ensure that personal relationships remain healthy. The more we recognise and deal with stress triggers, the less likely we are to relapse into depression.

## If, When And How To Disengage From Drug Therapy

Let's examine three common questions.

### Should I Stop The Course Of Antidepressants At All?

Many reach the nine-month mark feeling much better. They often attribute much of their recovery to their course of anti-depressants and are worried about coming off them. Their concern is that they will immediately relapse back into depression. In the vast majority of cases, a nine-month course of drug therapy is all that is required. The drugs have done their job, in combination with the other therapies already outlined.

If your depression pattern is such that you only get occasional bouts of depression, in general nine months will be all that is required. If this is the case, you should plan, in consultation with your doctor, to come off medication at this time. If you have a long history of relapsing depression (often after quite a short period off drug therapy), the situation may have to be reassessed. There is definitely a cohort of people (often coming from a strong family tradition of depression) who need to remain on a 'maintenance regimen of medication' for life.

While this is clearly not desirable, the reality for this group may be that, despite all other therapy approaches, maintenance drug therapy is necessary. It can be equated to those diabetics for whom diet alone is not sufficient and who have to accept that they need to follow drug therapy for life.

It is important to realise that these people form only about 20 to 25 percent of those who suffer from depression. Even within this group, many may have intermittent remissions, and can take a break from drug therapy during these remissions.

For the remainder, nine months is the ideal time to cease antidepressants. We will examine later the typical negative thoughts preventing many making this step – and how to deal with them.

### When Should I Stop Taking Antidepressants?

There is no hard-and-fast rule that we must stop taking antidepressants at any particular time. But experience has taught us that ceasing them between three and six months often leads to a relapse of depression.

If we have taken a course lasting eight or nine months, there is little to be gained in most cases by continuing with them. The exception, as outlined above, is the group who suffer from repeated successive bouts of depression. They should only stop taking them if they have had a long period free from illness – usually several years.

Some specialists will increase the period from nine to eighteen months in the case of a person who relapses very quickly after coming off a course of antidepressants for the first time. This, in my opinion, is a useful option, but only on condition that they have made the necessary lifestyle changes outlined and have also, through talk therapy, dealt with the issues outlined in the last chapter. Remember, drug therapy is an important part of the holistic treatment of depression, but it must be combined with the rest of the package in order to be truly effective.

## How Should We Stop Taking Antidepressants?

This is another area which is often badly managed. Most modern antidepressants are short-acting so have to be withdrawn slowly. Otherwise the patient may experience the 'discontinuation syndrome'. This is where the person on treatment suddenly ceases medication and the brain reacts to the absence of medication. They may get sensations of spinning, lack of balance and nausea, and generally feel unwell. This is instantly treatable by reintroducing the antidepressant; within hours, the symptoms will disappear. The main exceptions to this are the modern drugs Prozac (which takes a long time to be broken down in the body), valdoxan and Zispin, and some of the older antidepressants. When these drugs are withdrawn we do not experience any of the above symptoms. This discontinuation syndrome led many to assume that these drugs were addictive. In practice, it has nothing to do with addiction; it is more to do with suddenly withdrawing the drug from the brain. To avoid discontinuation syndrome, work with your family doctor to gradually reduce the strength of the drug over several weeks, before stopping it completely. This gives the brain the chance to readjust and avoid developing these symptoms.

## If, When And How To Disengage From Talk Therapy

While everybody considers disengaging from drug therapy to be a significant issue, few realise that disengaging from talk therapy can present similar difficulties. For those involved in an empathetic relationship with the family doctor or therapist who is assisting them on the journey, disengaging can bring on similar feelings of anxiety as with drug therapy. When we have got to nine months and are well, we may fear that without the therapist's support and encouragement, depression will once again return.

### Should I Stop The Course Of Talk Therapy At All?

The answer really lies in why you are receiving talk therapy to start with. We should stop talk therapy when we have dealt with the issues which are troubling us. If you still feel that there is work to be done, then continue until you are comfortable that you have dealt with them. I have come across some patients who have continued working with a therapist long after their depression has been treated. It is important for therapists as well as doctors to know when it is time to disengage.

CBT for negative thinking and ruminations, anxiety, hurt or shame will be able to deal with most of these issues within the first nine months. Apart from occasional top-ups, we should have ceased talk therapy by then.

If you are involved in significant therapy involving abuse or serious issues in your past, you may need a longer period. But it is important to set a definite timeframe for such work. If you have gone as far as you can, you should disengage.

If you feel that you are becoming dependent on your therapist, then consider disengaging. Remember that disengaging from your therapist does not mean that you break off the relationship. You leave open the possibility that if you get back into difficulties over some issues, you can return!

As with drug therapy, it is anxiety that prevents many from disengaging from talk therapy: the fear that depression will return. Later, we will see how Dr Bill advises us to deal with this fear.

### When Should One Disengage From Talk Therapy?

As with drug therapy, there are no hard-and-fast rules to assist us. In general, however, the nine-month landmark is not a bad one to observe. The vast majority of people with depression will have gained sufficient insight through talk therapy by then.

The main group who may need longer periods are those who have experienced serious abuse, particularly sexual abuse. There are other areas, such as addiction, eating disorders, and major relationship difficulties, that may also need more extensive therapy.

But unless these are an issue, nine months should be as long as it should take.

### How Should We Disengage From Talk Therapy?

As with drug therapy, it should be a planned, phased withdrawal from the talk therapy in question. You should decide at some stage in your course how long it should last. Try and stick to this timetable and, with your therapist, agree when you should disengage. It is advisable to extend periods between sessions just as it is with drug therapy. This makes it easier to disengage. If you feel that you are becoming dependent on your therapist, then make this known, and work on a planned withdrawal over time.

Once again, leave open the option of returning if you get back into difficulties. In the case of CBT, it has been shown that an occasional top-up may keep us on the straight and narrow!

## In Summary, At Nine Months

Our first job is to continue the lifestyle changes that assisted us in both feeling and getting better.

We then assess our drug therapy regimen, if relevant. In general, nine months is the ideal time in most cases to disengage from drug therapy. The exception is where we are dealing with more severe, persistent depression.

We then review if it is time to disengage from talk therapy. In general, nine months is as long as most people with depression will require. The exception is when we are dealing with serious issues in the past relating to abuse, post-traumatic stress disorder, addiction, and so on, when longer periods may be required.

Now let's revisit some of the group we met earlier and see how they put this into practice.

## Paul's Story (revisited)

We met Paul earlier in the book. He was twenty-seven and had suffered from depression for over ten years. He had been sexually abused by a close friend of the family at the age of nine but had never revealed it to his family. He eventually tried to take his own life and narrowly escaped dying. As you will remember, he began to attend Dr Bill. With a holistic package of exercise, nutrition and supplements, after two months he was feeling much better. He also ceased alcohol and involved his workplace in the process.

He then started the serious work of getting better. He did a lot of CBT work with Dr Bill in his battle with negative ruminations, and this began to bear fruit.

Then he was ready to deal with the monster which had been gnawing at his insides from the age of nine: sexual abuse. On Dr Bill's advice, he began to attend a specialist therapist for abuse. He found this process to be incredibly traumatic and emotionally draining. But with the help of Dr Bill, and his partner Sandra, he began to make good progress.

By nine months he was both feeling a lot better and was genuinely on the road to getting well. At this point, he is now back with Dr Bill and is wondering if it is time to cease medication and talk therapies!

In this particular situation, Dr Bill is more cautious, however. He is concerned at both the length of duration of Paul's depression, and its severity. He is also uneasy that Paul has not yet fully dealt with his abuse.

So they decide, in this case, to continue the lifestyle changes and extend the period for antidepressants to eighteen months. He is also concerned that Paul deal fully with his previous abuse and wants him to continue seeing the therapist in this area.

So in this case, the decision at nine months is unusual in that Paul is advised to continue with both drug and talk therapy for another nine months. Later, we will see how he fares.

## Mary's Story (revisited)

We also met Mary earlier in the book. She is twenty-nine and a highly successful businesswoman who has been living with her long-term boyfriend for over five years. You may recall that she became depressed following a series of life events. Her sister's son takes his own life and Mary ends up supporting her through this tragedy. Due to the recession, her workload increases. Her partner is placed on a three-day week and they run into financial difficulties. She eventually takes an overdose and, luckily, survives.

She ends up with Dr Bill. He manages, with the usual holistic package, including antidepressants, to assist her in feeling better by eight weeks and then begins the task of helping her get better.

Firstly, they decide to take her off work until she is feeling better and to continue her holistic therapy package. He then helps her challenge her negative rumination, in particular her deep-seated belief that she is worthless. They do a number of 'ABC's on different situations where she finds herself rating herself.

Dr Bill then advises her and her partner to visit a business advisor to deal with their financial difficulties. This goes a long way towards lifting the burden of seemingly overwhelming debt, and they restructure their financial affairs.

By nine months, she is both feeling and getting better. She attends Dr Bill and, after reviewing her case, he feels that she in now ready to move on. He firstly suggests that she continue with her exercise, nutrition, supplement and financial advisor, but also that it might be time to consider coming off her medication. She reacts badly to the suggestion that her antidepressants might cease. Dr Bill decides to do an 'ABC' with her on the issue.

A: Activating Event
- Trigger: The decision to cease antidepressants at nine months
- Inference/danger If she stops medication, her depression may recur. If this happens, she will be unable to cope and would be upset with herself for allowing it to happen.

B: Belief/Demand
- That she must be completely certain (if ceasing drug therapy) that her depression will not recur.

C: Consequences
- Emotion: Anxiety
- Physical Symptoms: The usual symptoms of anxiety
- Behaviour: She tries to avoid the situation by trying to persuade Dr Bill that she still needs her medication. She ruminates on the possibility of her depression returning, how awful this will be, and how she won't be able to cope. She seeks out the opinion of her boyfriend, looking for confirmation that she is right in her concern about depression returning if medication ceases.

Dr Bill explains that this is one of the commonest pitfalls that many recovering from depression fall into. They become incredibly anxious that if medication is stopped, their depression will recur.

He and Mary agree that her behavioural responses are not helping the situation and only increasing her anxiety. They could also argue about whether her interpretation of what will happen when ceasing drug therapy could be wrong. But this would be pointless, as it is impossible to predict one way or the other.

He therefore challenges her demand that she must be completely certain that her depression will not return if she ceases medication. In practice, is anything in life 100 percent certain? She would have to accept that there was always going to be a chance that depression could recur, irrespective of whether she was on drug therapy or not. She was also catastrophising – creating in her own mind the worst-case scenario – without any evidence to back it up. But the real key was in her statement that she would not be able to cope if her depression returned. We all feel that we will not cope with so many things in life, but when they happen, we do cope. This is because it is in our own interests, and in the interests of those we love, to cope.

Mary finally realises that she is really trying to control life and that this is not possible for any of us. She accepts that she has to live with the possibility that her depression could recur, but also that she would be able to cope if it did. That is not to say that she would not do everything in her power to reduce the chances of this happening!

We will see how things develop later.

## Siobhan's Story (revisited)

We met Siobhan earlier as well. She was twenty-eight, and had had a baby five months before. A classical perfectionist, she liked everything to be in order, particularly in relation to her house, and her work as a high-powered secretary to a business executive.

She had struggled with the trauma of a new baby arriving in her nicely organised world and could not accept that she was (unlike 'all her friends who had babies') not coping!

She goes on to develop classical signs of postnatal depression and has thoughts of self-harm, which add guilt to her heavy emotional load. She is also struggling to bond with her baby.

She ends up visiting Dr Bill, who initially recommends a simple holistic package of exercise, nutrition, supplements, ceasing alcohol, and so on, aimed at lifting her mood. Her mood falls further and she eventually begins a course of anti-depressants, which help her (along with the other lifestyle changes) to feel better.

After eight weeks, they begin the task of helping her to get better. Dr Bill works with her on negative thoughts and explains why so many women get into trouble to begin with. In a nutshell, they are not prepared for the turbulence which follows the arrival a new baby into the house.

Suddenly the mothers (and fathers) are faced with no sleep, and constant concerns about doing the right thing in relation to the child's diet and health. The child usually cries, for numerous reasons, from colic to teething. The mother becomes exhausted and the father feels shut out. Sex drive plummets in the female (but not so much in the male), which leads to further difficulties. It is like one long nightmare that seems as if it will never end. And that is only year one!

While this is a normal phenomenon for most mothers, the difficulty is that many feel that they, not the situation, are the problem. They berate themselves for not coping and eventually end up getting depressed.

Once Siobhan, as a result of working with Dr Bill, realises that 'it is the situation that is abnormal, not her', she begins to reshape her approach to the whole area. Her mood, thinking and behaviour all change for the better.

Dr Bill then begins to work with Siobhan on her anxiety. For as soon as her depression lifted, symptoms of anxiety came back. They begin to do 'ABC's on many common triggers for her anxiety. One of the commonest for her was her fear that something will happen to her baby and that, as a result, he will die. This fear was most often triggered when watching TV while the child is asleep. Dr Bill does an 'ABC' with her on this:

A: Activating Event
- Trigger: Watching TV when child asleep
- Inference/danger: That because she is not there, she might find the child dead due to a cot death. If this happened, she would never be able to forgive herself and would not be able to cope.

B: Belief/Demand
- That she must be completely certain her baby will not die as a result of a cot death.

C: Consequences
- Emotion: Anxiety
- Physical Symptoms: The usual symptoms of anxiety
- Behaviour: She spent most of her time hovering over the baby, even when the baby is asleep. She struggles to let the baby out of her sight. If her husband is the one looking after the baby when she is not there, she rings him constantly to make sure all is well. She brings the child to the doctor with the slightest symptom and checks the internet regularly to make sure she is not missing anything. She also constantly ruminates on how awful it would be if something did happen.

Dr Bill challenges her behaviour, and they agree that her constant 'hovering' is only increasing her anxiety, making it more likely that her depression would recur. They agree that the hovering is also completely counterproductive, as it cannot prevent such an incident actually happening.

But he spends most of his time helping her to challenge the demand for 100 percent certainty that her baby must not die from cot death. Of course, like any sensible mother, she would prefer that such a tragedy would not occur, but there were no certainties in relation to this, or any other area of life. She had to learn to live with the tiny chance that her baby might get ill for any reason, including cot death. In real life, although these were possibilities, in practice they were very rare occurrences. He challenged her desire for 100 percent certainty in other areas of her life.

He challenged her catastrophising: assuming that the worst case scenario would occur. Had she any proof that her baby was definitely the one that was going to die? Where was her proof that this was the case, or was it in fact only her emotional mind playing tricks with her. He challenges her belief that she would not cope: in real life she would, because it would be in her interests to do so.

He also challenges her belief that if something actually happened to her baby, this would mean that she was a complete failure. How could some freak illness to her baby make her a failure anyway?

By doing a number of 'ABC's in this manner, Dr Bill helps Siobhan learn to deal with her anxiety. This is the last chain in her journey towards getting better.

At nine months, Siobhan is now back with Dr Bill and ready for the next step: learning how to stay well. He encourages her to continue her lifestyle changes but takes her off medication. It is also important that she start to disengage from him from the point of view of talk therapy. She has learned a great deal and now needs to start putting it into practice on her own. Later, we will see how she fares!

## From One Year Onwards

We have now dealt with that critical period from nine months up to one year, and our journey is nearly at its end. The last part is to learn how to stay well from one year onwards.

We will examine this under a number of headings:

- What is the role of lifestyle in staying well?
- What is the role of drug therapy in staying well?
- What is the role of talk therapy in staying well?
- What is the role of self-help groups, websites, volunteering and community work in staying well?
- What is the role of mindfulness in staying well?
- What is the role of creative therapy in staying well?
- What, if any, is the role of spirituality in staying well?

We will see from this list just how widely we have to cast the net in our quest to stay well. The best chance of achieving this objective is to open ourselves up to such a menu. As a general rule, the more work we have put in on our journey to date, the easier it will be to put what we have learned into practice.

For each person, the cocktail of measures will be different – because we are all unique and special human beings. There will, however, be some measures that I will be recommending for everyone, as these have been found to be useful in staying well.

## What Is The Role Of Lifestyle In Staying Well?

This is an important foundation stone if you are serious about keeping depression at bay. Many who relapse let this area slide. We have examined lifestyle regularly up to this point, but let's, for the last time, summarise the main areas.

### Exercise

This is probably the most important anti-relapse measure. The constant mantra of thirty minutes a day of any form of exercise, quoted so often in this book, remains the gold standard. Ideally, the exercise should occur out in the fresh air, as sunlight is also very helpful for mood. If we can involve somebody to accompany us each day, so much the better – as this adds a social dimension, which has a positive impact on mental health.

### Nutrition

Again, nutrition is important in our battle to stay well. Try and keep to a healthy diet of fruit, vegetables, fish, lean meat and nuts, and avoid high-sugar foods and drinks and stimulants like coffee.

## Supplements
These are a useful adjunct to the above. Although claims are made for many supplements, I would recommend simply continuing your Omega 3 fish oils and B complex vitamins.

## Alcohol
This will remain, for most people struggling to stay well, a substance that will need constant monitoring in their lives. When well again, the temptation is to allow it back into our lives in amounts that may not be healthy. It is a good idea to set the weekly levels at the beginning and try not to go over them. The levels in question should ideally not exceed the safety levels of fourteen units for women and twenty-one for men.

But if your mood falls for a few days after alcohol, then consider taking alcohol out of the picture altogether. Each person must find what level they can, or can't, take and be honest with themselves about the effects alcohol has on *them*.

## Substance Abuse And Misuse
Like alcohol, this is important to face if it is an issue in your life. It is unlikely that you will have got to the stage of getting the better of your depression if you have not faced up to this addiction earlier on the journey. But there may be some who are now well again and may fall into the trap of assuming that it is now possible to start taking the substance again. That will be the rock on which they will perish. Others may not have been honest from the beginning: if so, then now is the time to do so. Be sure to seek out professional and self-help groups if you are travelling this road.

Remember that this also includes more subtle substance abuse, like addiction to over-the-counter medications such as codeine and legal substances like tranquillisers.

## Monitoring Stress

This is an absolutely crucial part of staying well. As detailed on countless occasions in this book, stress is often the trigger for a fresh bout of depression. But as we all know, stress is endemic to our lives – so how can we prevent it? The key is to examine, weekly, any significant issues causing us concern – whether they relate to finances, employment, relationships or family problems. Write them down and then see if there is anything practical that can be done to reduce their impact. If necessary, seek help – from family members, or in the form of financial advice or counselling – if you are struggling to deal with them on your own. I would also advise readers to read my book *Toxic Stress* to examine the whole area of stress in more detail.

## What Is The Role Of Drug Therapy In Staying Well?

This is not an issue for the majority of people recovering from depression, because most of these people will have ceased taking them after around nine months. For this group, drug therapy has no further role in their battle to stay well.

But there is a smaller group, of around 20 percent of sufferers, who may have to build drug therapy in as part of their longer-term depression-prevention plans. In some cases, they may have to stay on this course for a further one to two years, and in other cases for life.

There are two main types of drug therapy used for the prevention of further bouts of depression:

Antidepressants form the main group. As already detailed, they usually belong to the modern SSRI or SRNI type. Some people only stay well if they are left on a maintenance dose for life. In such cases, the dose should be brought down to the minimum required for this purpose.

It is not the ideal that anyone should have to continue taking drugs for life. If you ask anyone with diabetes or high blood pressure whether they are happy having to take drugs, the answer is usually negative. But they take them because the consequences of not doing so outweigh their dislike of having to take them.

If you belong to this group, you have probably had numerous bouts of depression and are tired of battling them. If, as part of a total package of measures, drug therapy is helping you then accept that it may have to stay.

The risk of relapse occurs when, if you are part of this group, you make a unilateral decision to stop taking them. You may do this for countless reasons, but mostly they are related to other people's views on antidepressants, and possible side effects. I exhort you always to talk the issue out with your doctor before taking this step. If not, the danger is that you may trigger a new bout of major depression and have to begin all over again!

Mood stabilisers are the second main group. This will only be relevant to a much smaller group who have struggled both to treat their bouts of depression and to prevent relapses. In general, they will be attending a psychiatrist due to the severity of episodes, and there may be a family history of significant depression or even bipolar disorder.

We detail some of these in the appendix. Suffice to say that if they are helping, then please continue taking them. Just one word of caution for women of child-bearing age: if you are on these drugs and thinking of getting pregnant, discuss it first with your doctor or psychiatrist. This is because some of these drugs may carry a risk to the baby.

## What Is The Role Of Talk Therapy In Staying Well?

Once again, we hope that by one year you have dealt with the main issues that triggered your depression bout and have learned how to deal with the negative ruminations of depression. Most will at this stage have disengaged from their therapist or doctor in terms of talk therapy.

But there are a few situations where talk therapy can be very useful in our drive to stay well.

### Supportive Talk Therapy

This can be important for some people recovering from a bout of depression. This may take the form of occasional meetings to see how you are getting on, and perhaps to consolidate areas you will have both worked on in your journey towards getting well. As long as you do not feel that such contact is a crutch on which you have become dependent, this can be extremely helpful.

## Talk Therapy For Abuse Or Significant Traumas

This can, on occasion, last for a lot longer than one year. It can be a long, traumatic, painful exercise to deal with complex areas like abuse. It is important to deal with such issues, no matter how long it takes, or how difficult it might be. The reward is that we are less likely to suffer a relapse of depression.

## CBT

CBT can, on occasion, also assist us on our journey towards staying well. You may have already done some significant work on negative ruminations and behaviour in depression. You may also have received some assistance in how to deal with anxiety, hurt or guilt. Sometimes matters will arise in your life that may relate to this, and returning for assistance for a single visit on occasions may sort them out. This may prevent the person from spiralling back down into a negative vortex ending up with depression.

## Relationship Or Addiction Talk Therapy

This can also take longer than the one year allocated. This is because issues can keep turning up that we struggle with. It is better to return for assistance from your therapist in such situations rather than letting things slide.

In all cases, as long as you find that the talk therapy intervention is helping you deal with issues and move on in life, I encourage you to continue. If you are not finding it particularly helpful or feel dependent on the therapist in order to survive, then I counsel caution. You may be doing more harm than good.

Remember, the whole role of talk therapy is to have you standing on your own two feet with a good understanding of the issues affecting your life. When you reach this stage, your chances of a depression relapse will diminish significantly.

## What Is The Role Of Self-Help Groups, Websites, Volunteering And Community Work In Staying Well?

We now move to looking at mental health in a wider setting. Many with depression who have travelled the journey back to health like to help others. This can be a powerful and often overlooked tool in our desire to stay well. Man is not meant to be alone. The more we interact with and involve ourselves with others in the community, the healthier we will remain. Let's examine how this might work in action.

## Self-Help Groups

Self-help groups can be a great source of support for people with depression, addiction and the whole gamut of mental health difficulties. There are many such groups, both at local and national level. There are also excellent groups on university and college campuses. If you have recovered from your bout of depression, then think about putting your name forward to help. This may involve personal involvement in such groups, working on a telephone helpline, fundraising or media work. It doesn't matter how small your involvement is – you will feel better for doing it. There is a list of such groups at the back of this book with contact details.

## Websites

Websites of many self-help groups like Aware are starting online support groups, and this is another area you can volunteer to help with. You may find such work extremely rewarding.

## Volunteering And Community Work

This is another way to improve our mental health while helping others. This may involve volunteering to help with our environment, visiting those who are elderly and need assistance, working with young people at sport or community level, or sharing our skills with groups that help the disadvantaged. The more you share with others, the more positive you will feel about yourself and the less likely you are to suffer a relapse of depression.

## What Is The Role Of Mindfulness In Staying Well?

There has been great interest in mindfulness in the past decade as a tool to assist us in reducing depression relapse. It is not a good idea to involve ourselves with this therapy at the beginning, as it may make matters worse.

But there is increasing evidence that, when we have recovered from our bout, developing mindfulness skills can be useful in preventing depression. People in the East have been using mindfulness and meditation for over five thousand years, mainly through Buddhist practices. It is one of the core components of yoga, for example. Recently, scientists and therapists in the West have been examining these approaches to see if they can play a role in preventing depression and managing stress.

MINDFULNESS is the awareness which develops when we pay attention to events experienced in the present moment within the framework of our mind/body in a non-judgemental and accepting manner. This is being increasingly recognised as a very useful tool for those who are so distressed by negative emotions that they struggle to come to terms with the negative thoughts lying beneath. Tony Bates, founder of Headstrong, has been a champion of this approach in treating depression and other mental health difficulties.

Mindfulness:

- assists us in noticing 'what is happening in our experience' (especially when engaging in compulsive patterns of thought, such as rumination);
- offers a way for people to 'stay with experiences', including whatever may be unpleasant or difficult, rather than pushing them away;
- produces a change in our perspective on those thoughts or experiences, enabling people to see that their thoughts are just thoughts, not facts or reality, and that they need not be driven by them;
- allows 'choice'. Rather than us being driven by compulsive reactions to experience, mindfulness creates the mental space that enables people to respond differently; helps us move from the 'world of doing' to the 'world of being'.

Mindfulness has been partially absorbed into the world of CBT, where a form of meditation called 'mindfulness-based cognitive therapy' (MBCT) has been developed. This therapy links the principles behind CBT to mindfulness.

I would like to pick out one wonderful mindfulness exercise that is often used in MBCT and is of particular use in depression, but can be of benefit to anyone: the 'three-minute breathing space'.

It can be done at any time of the day, particularly if the person is under a lot of stress, and involves finding a quiet space, and if possible a comfortable posture, closing your eyes, and engaging with the following:

MINUTE ONE

Focus our mind on inner experiences – whether it is our thoughts, emotions and physical sensations. Do not try to change or challenge them, just become aware of them.

MINUTE TWO

Focus on the simple physical sensation of 'breathing', particularly on your abdomen rising and falling with each breath, again not trying in any way to 'control' it. This helps 'centre' us.

MINUTE THREE

Increase focus or awareness of the body as a whole, including posture, facial expressions and sensations present, with acceptance and without judgement.

This is often called a 'mini-meditation'. If it is performed two or three times a day, the benefits are enormous. It is also a simple approach, for those who do not want to travel the full meditation/mindfulness route. I would encourage everyone recovering from depression to build this into their life as a daily routine.

## What Is The Role Of Creative Therapy In Staying Well?

For some people, the creative arts are an area where they can express their emotions. Many who suffer from depression can find great peace in painting, music, craftwork, pottery, poetry, theatre and literature. There is some evidence that involving ourselves in creative arts can be self-soothing, and a bulwark against depression. This will take a different form for each person, depending on their interests.

If you are interested in any of these areas, it might be worth pursuing them further. Like mindfulness, we can let go of many of our negative thoughts and emotions in this way. These arts often have an added social dimension, which can also be nourishing to our mood.

## What, If Any, Is The Role Of Spirituality In Staying Well?

We live in a world where spirituality is constantly confused with religion. One is a search for meaning, and the other is a system of beliefs. Many struggle to find meaning in their lives in our modern scientific world, which is dominated by information technology and news media.

I have always been a great fan of the late John O'Donoghue and loved the way he was able to see spirituality in the beautiful landscape of the Burren and Connemara and in the simplicity of human relationships. He and others have quite rightly castigated the evils that exist within some of the religious structures which have, on occasions, oppressed those they serve. But that has not stopped John and like-minded individuals from finding beauty, meaning and spirituality in their lives.

But there is now a vacuum in many people's lives that they are struggling to fill. Is this relevant to mental health? I believe that it is. Each person must find their own path in this area, but if you are trying to stay well, I would encourage you at least to examine this area. There is evidence that those who find some spiritual meaning in their lives, in whatever form, are more resilient to stress and anxiety, and less prone to bouts of depression.

# PART SEVEN

## How They Fared

### Gerry's Story (revisited)

We met Gerry in earlier chapters; here, we will summarise his progress. Gerry had suffered significant depression in his first two years in college. Matters came to a head in his third year, when he decided to take his own life. He was saved by a call to a college helpline. He began to attend Dr Bill, who laid out a holistic programme for him involving exercise, nutrition and supplements, a dawn simulator and ceasing alcohol. He began a course of antidepressants and became involved in a self-help group. His college assisted him in taking a break from his studies in order to reduce his immediate stress. Now Dr Bill began to assist him in the area of the negative thinking using the 'ABC' method.

He then referred him for therapy to deal with issues relating to his childhood and upbringing. The last major block was to learn how to deal with the longstanding hurt stemming from childhood experiences; Dr Bill assisted him in this with some CBT exercises. As a result of this session, Gerry made a breakthrough: he decided that this hurt had done him enough damage in his life. He ended up dropping the hurt and forgiving his father.

After nine months, Gerry was off his antidepressants, was continuing his holistic lifestyle changes and had taken up mindfulness. Over the next four years, Gerry continued to do well. He married Jane, who was now working in media, and the couple had two children. He managed to find employment and worked hard at managing stress in his life. He continued to improve his relationship with his family, particularly his father. To date, he has stayed well:

he has had no further bouts of depression. He disengaged from Dr Bill after ten months but occasionally returns for some CBT top-ups if he runs into situations he finds difficult to manage.

## Dr Bill's Comments

Gerry has worked hard on his depression, changing many aspects of his life. If we were to summarise his progress through our four steps, it would look like this:

STEP 1: Gerry comes to accept that he has depression through a near-suicide attempt and liaison with self-help groups and counsellors. He then decides to attend Dr Bill.

STEP 2: Through an eight-week holistic package of exercise, nutrition, supplements, ceasing alcohol, dawn simulator and reducing stress in his life, combined with a course of anti-depressants, he is now feeling much better!

STEP 3: From three to nine months, he does a lot of talk therapy while continuing with his holistic therapy. In particular, he does some CBT on negative rumination, some counselling on dealing with difficulties in his past, and some further CBT work on dealing with deep-seated hurt.

STEP 4: From nine months onwards, he ceases his antidepressants, consolidates his lifestyle changes, begins to study mindfulness and continues to work on his thinking and his tendency to rate himself.

## Siobhan's Story (revisited)

We met Siobhan earlier; we will summarise her story to date. She had a history of anxiety and developed postnatal depression at around five months after the birth of her baby.

She ends up visiting Dr Bill, who initially tries to lift her mood using a simple holistic package that includes exercise, nutrition, supplements and ceasing alcohol. But her mood falls further and she eventually agrees to begin a course of antidepressants. This, along with the other lifestyle changes, helps her to feel better by eight weeks.

Between three and nine months, Siobhan begins to tackle the thinking and behavioural problems associated with her depression by using talk therapy. She learns that almost all women suffer from significant stress, and that many struggle to cope in the year after giving birth. She begins to accept that it is the situation that is abnormal, not her, and changes her approach.

As she is improving further, Dr Bill starts to work with her on her anxiety. They do some CBT exercises using the 'ABC' system, which she finds very helpful. After nine months, Siobhan is off her drug therapy and continues to be very careful with her lifestyle programme.

Two years on, she remains well and has taken up yoga: she finds both the physical and mindfulness exercises extremely helpful in her life.

### Dr Bill's Comments

Siobhan has also worked hard on understanding the issues underlying her depression. If we were to summarise her progress through our four steps, it would look like this:

STEP 1: Siobhan, with some reluctance, comes to accept that she has developed postnatal depression. She chooses Dr Bill to be her guide.

STEP 2: She, through an eight week holistic package of exercise, nutrition, supplements, ceasing alcohol and trying to get assistance to deal with stress in her life; combined with a course of antidepressants is now feeling much better!

STEP 3: From three to nine months, she involves herself with talk therapy while continuing with her holistic therapy. She learns to accept that many women will experience a somewhat chaotic year following the birth of their baby. She uses CBT to deal with her negative ruminations and longstanding difficulties with anxiety.

STEP 4: From nine months, she ceases her antidepressants, consolidates her lifestyle changes, and takes up yoga.

Two years later, Siobhan continues to improve, but obviously any further pregnancies, with their potentially explosive combination of hormonal changes and stress, may make her vulnerable to further bouts of depression. However, the work she has done on her thinking and behaviour should reduce the risks of this happening.

She will also find that the CBT work on her chronic anxiety will bear fruit for the rest of her life. She also understands the reality of life with a newborn baby!

## Jim's Story (revisited)

Unfortunately, Jim didn't make it. Jim spent a decade living in the dark world of depression and despair. He came from a family where his mother and two brothers had suffered from significant bouts of major depression. Jim was extremely bright and advanced quickly through college and less than three years after joining a multinational company, he was made head of a division.

However, his depression was deteriorating and he was misusing alcohol, and eventually he began to consider suicide. He opens up to his doctor while under investigation for fatigue and ends up being referred to Dr Bill, who applies a holistic package, including a course of antidepressants. Jim is extremely reluctant either to exercise or to take medication. But with Dr Bill's advice and support, he agrees.

Eight weeks later, he is feeling better for the first time in years, with an improvement in mood, fatigue, sleep and concentration. His suicide thoughts begin to wane. He is exercising and avoiding alcohol completely. With the support of his company, he takes a two-month break from his high-stress job.

Between three and nine months, Jim, with the assistance of Dr Bill, starts to challenge his negative thinking and behaviour using the 'ABC' system. In particular, Dr Bill challenges Jim's view that he is worthless. He helps Jim see that these are just words that we use and that they may have no basis in reality.

By nine months, and after a lot of CBT and support from Dr Bill, Jim is getting better. He is anxious to come off drug therapy, and Dr Bill agrees to give him a trial off it. Jim is very conscientious about his lifestyle changes, in particular exercise. He has stayed off alcohol, as he felt better without it. By one year, Jim has made a good recovery and all is going well.

A year later, Jim's company moves him to a different part of the country. He meets Theresa, a primary school teacher, with whom he falls in love. She becomes pregnant but unfortunately ends up having a miscarriage at eleven weeks. It is a devastating blow to both of them. Theresa becomes very down, and the relationship breaks up. Jim struggles to cope with the breakdown of the relationship. His mood starts to fall. He begins to drink again as a coping mechanism and his sleep pattern deteriorates. He loses weight and his work performance begins to suffer. One of the problems he faces is that he is a long way away from his family and his few close friends. He stops exercising and begins to spend more and more time on his computer on suicide sites. Back came the original bleak thoughts. The bleak thoughts he had experienced years before, during his last bout of depression, return:

- 'I can't see any hope for myself.'
- 'Maybe it would be for the best if I was simply not around.'
- 'I just can't go on.'

Occasionally, he thought of travelling back to see Dr Bill again. But his emotional mind quickly overruled this:

- 'What would be the point: there's nothing he could do to help.'
- 'It's too late.'
- 'It's just me.'

Eventually he is spending more and more time on the internet, investigating ways of taking his own life. Finally he makes his decision. He rings everybody he loves, including his mother. To them, he seems to be in great form. He tells Theresa and his mum how much he loves them. He writes two notes: one to his family and one to Theresa. Jim was found two days later in his apartment; he had died by suicide.

*Dr Bill's Comments*

Jim's story is particularly tragic. Let's examine, firstly, how he dealt with his bout of depression through the usual four-step process, and then what happened subsequently.

STEP 1: Jim comes to accept, with the help of his doctor, that he has depression. He then decides to attend Dr Bill.

STEP 2: He, through an eight week holistic package of exercise, nutrition, supplements, ceasing alcohol, and reducing stress in his life; combined with a course of antidepressants is now feeling much better. He also begins a course of antidepressants. After the eight weeks has passed, he is feeling better.

STEP 3: From three to nine months, Jim does a lot of talk therapy, while continuing with his holistic therapy. He does some CBT on negative ruminations and unhelpful behavior.

STEP 4: From nine months onwards, he ceases his antidepressants, consolidates his lifestyle changes, particularly exercise, and continues to work on his negative thoughts and his tendency to rate himself. By this stage, he is doing well and has disengaged from Dr Bill.

So what went wrong in Jim's life that led to his suicide? The key is that Jim had a history of significant major depression in his past and was always going to be susceptible to the arrival of serious stress in his life.

The first big stress was that he had moved away from his family, support structures and friends. He had also taken on a new job, with all the stresses that this can entail.

The major stress was his partner's miscarriage and the subsequent breakdown of the relationship. Men frequently struggle with relationship breakdowns, and in this case there was a double 'bereavement'. The stress of this, added to his predisposition to depression, led to his mood falling.

This led to a breakdown in the lifestyle changes he had so carefully cultivated

– in particular stopping exercise and restarting alcohol. These led to his mood dropping further and the negative thoughts pouring in. Once the extremely unhelpful information emanating from the website promoting suicide is added in, disaster was inevitable.

What Jim couldn't see in his dark, bleak world of pain was the depth of pain he was about to inflict on all those who loved them. His mother had a major heart attack one year later and passed away, due to stress associated with Jim's death.

He also couldn't see that, although the problems in his life were painful, time and counselling could have helped him deal with them. As he had already seen, his depression was treatable, using the four-step process.

Suicide can be seen as a permanent solution to temporary problems thrown up by life. So if anyone is reading this and contemplating suicide, remember that there is a much easier way to manage your pain: come forward and open up about how you feel! It is also crucial to avoid websites which do not have your best interests at heart. At the back of this book are contact numbers for some of the many groups that exist to help people in Jim's situation.

## Kate's Story (revisited)

We also met Kate earlier in the book. You may remember how she was physically and sexually abused by her alcoholic father, and later found herself in a relationship with a similarly abusive partner. She had a three-year-old child and relied on her partner to help rear him. She had started off with panic attacks secondary to being anxious due to the abuse she was receiving, and then became severely depressed. She was getting serious suicide thoughts that it might be better if she and her baby were no longer around. She ends up in A&E following a broken jaw – the result of an assault by her partner. There she meets a social worker who passes her on to see Dr Bill. Her journey has begun. By the time she reaches him, her mood is extremely low. Her child is now in temporary foster care. At least Kate is now in a place of safety, where her abusive partner cannot assault her. Dr Bill institutes a holistic package of exercise, nutrition, supplements and avoiding alcohol. He starts her on an antidepressant, to be prescribed weekly until her suicidal thoughts have settled.

He also encourages her to stay in the hostel and to separate completely from her abusive partner.

The next six weeks are a real battle for Kate, but slowly her mood starts to lift and her appetite, sleep, energy and concentration improve. The suicide thoughts, which had reached the planning stage, start to subside. She seeks, and is granted, a protection order against her partner, and presses charges against him. She is able to see her child for short periods under supervision.

By eight weeks, she is feeling much better and is ready to face the serious challenges that will arise in her battle to become well again. Dr Bill encourages her to stay on the regimen as outlined. He points out that it is now time for Kate, through talk therapy, to start to sort out various key issues in her life.

Her immediate stress triggers are the temporary loss of her child and the fear that her former partner will find out where she is living and seriously assault her. Dr Bill encourages her to continue down the legal route in relation to her former partner and to work with her social worker in relation to her child. He then turns his attention to her negative thinking: Kate still feels that she is completely worthless and not worth saving. It is only her child that keeps her going.

The years of abuse at the hands of her alcoholic father and then her partner has left its mark. She feels that she deserves to be treated in such a manner. Dr Bill takes the view that she will need counselling and refers her to a therapist who specialises in sexual abuse.

By eight months, Kate is thriving and has her baby back. With the help of her social worker, she has moved into a new flat and her former partner has ceased to be a problem. She finds the therapy sessions in relation to her abuse extremely difficult and often ends up distressed and in tears after them. But bit by bit, she is learning new ways to cope with her past.

However, there is still one important area with which she continues to have difficulty. This is the hurt and anger she is carrying towards her mother, who had failed to protect her. As a result of her therapy, she was able to deal with the anger she felt towards her father but struggled to deal with her emotions in relation to her mother. She returns to Dr Bill, seeking his help.

Dr Bill is delighted with her overall progress. Her mood has now returned to normal and her suicide thoughts have become a thing of the past. She has put on weight and is happily bonding with her child. She has done a lot of good work with her therapist but Dr Bill knows that if she continues to carry this hurt towards her mother, it would return in the future and would cause her difficulties. He does an 'ABC' on her hurt and she makes a major breakthrough in this area.

After a year, Kate is doing really well. She is off medication and has disengaged from her therapist. She has continued her lifestyle changes and has even signed up to do the women's marathon. She is very careful with her nutrition, alcohol intake and stress triggers.

She has started to socialise again and is in a new relationship, this time with a man who cares about her. She is also giving something back for all the help she has received: she works at the hostel on a voluntary basis. She now has a positive relationship with her mother, and both of them are benefiting from this new situation.

Three years later she remains well: she is married to her new partner and is expecting her second child.

## Dr Bill's Comments

Kate's story is a classical example of the damage that abuse in all its forms (particularly sexual abuse) can cause. Many who come from this background end up with major depression in their adult lives. On occasions, such depression can be quite resistant to treatment unless it comes to the surface and is dealt with. Unfortunately, it is also common for the sufferer of such abuse to end up in a relationship with a partner with similar abusive traits.

Kate had travelled this path and was fortunate to have been picked up in A&E before her depression reached a critical stage and a suicide attempt occurred. She was also able to access help from a number of agencies, which helped her seek out help.

She was also ready, at eight weeks of holistic therapy, to begin talk therapy aimed at dealing with her abusive past and present. The most important step was for her to deal with the hurt – towards her mother – that was eating her up inside. The CBT help that she received helped her deal with this hurt. She is now working hard at staying well.

If we were to chart her story in a four-step process, it would go as follows:

STEP 1: Kate ends up in A&E following a physical assault. With the help of a social worker and the hostel, she ends up with Dr Bill as her guide.

STEP 2: She, through an eight week holistic package of exercise, nutrition, supplements, ceasing alcohol, and reducing stress in her life; combined with a course of antidepressants is now feeling much better!

In particular she leaves her abusive partner, puts her child into temporary care and gets assistance from a local hostel. She also begins a course of antidepressants. By the end of this phase, she is feeling better.

STEP 3: From three to nine months, she does a lot of talk therapy, while continuing her holistic therapy. In particular, he does some counselling for her sexual abuse and CBT on her long-standing hurt. She forgives her mother.

STEP 4: From nine months onwards, she ceases antidepressants, consolidates her lifestyle changes (particularly exercise) and continues to work on her negative thinking and her tendency to rate herself. At this stage, she is doing well and has disengaged from Dr Bill.

## Paul's Story (revisited)

We met Paul on two occasions earlier in the book. He was twenty-seven and had suffered from depression for more than ten years. He had been sexually abused by a close friend of the family at the age of nine but had never revealed this to his family. He eventually tried to take his own life and had narrowly escaped dying. He began to attend Dr Bill, who through a holistic package of exercise, nutrition, supplement and antidepressants helped him reach a stage where, after two months, he was feeling much better. He also ceased alcohol and involved his workplace in his recovery from depression.

He moved on to the next phase, which incorporated talk therapy. This involved CBT with Dr Bill on his negative ruminations and with a specialist therapist in the area of the sexual abuse he had experienced. At nine months, even though he is both feeling and getting better, he continues, with Dr Bill's advice, with both drug and talk therapy.

This proves to be very wise advice: Paul had a few difficult periods as he continued to deal with the original abuse. He finally stopped medication two years after starting them; he continued to attend his therapist and Dr Bill throughout this period.

When he ceased medication, Paul stayed well but found that he struggled to deal with his constant negative ruminations and had to return regularly to Dr Bill for further CBT assistance. Dr Bill was concerned that he might go back into major depression. He enrolled Paul in a mindfulness course, which Paul found to be extremely helpful. He began to practise mindfulness on a daily basis. He also worked hard on his lifestyle changes, particularly exercise.

Two years later, he has remained well and is engaged to Sandra. He is aware, from his work with Dr Bill, that he remains at high risk for further bouts of depression. However, Sandra has a good understanding of depression and how it can affect Paul – and is a great support to him if he is having a bad day. He feels ready to help others and has begun working with a local voluntary suicide prevention group – sharing his own experiences with others.

## Dr Bill's Comments

Paul's story is one of great hope. He was lucky to have survived the suicide attempt – when, as you may remember, he had to be resuscitated. Once again the monster of sexual abuse lay hidden in his past. Its effects on Paul led to him developing significant major depression and almost cost him his life. He responded well to the usual holistic package but needed a longer course of both drug and talk therapy to deal with his underlying negative thinking and abusive past.

Paul will have to work hard at staying well, however. He will always struggle with his negative thoughts, which have become ingrained in his emotional brain. He has found mindfulness to be helpful in keeping these thoughts in check. He will also have to ensure that he keeps a watchful eye on lifestyle – particularly in the area of exercise.

If, despite all his hard work, Paul ends up relapsing into further bouts of depression, there would be an argument for him to take drug therapy for life, in view of his history, but one hopes that he will avoid this possibility.

We can summarise Paul's journey in our four-step process:

STEP 1: After surviving a serious suicide attempt, Paul comes to accept that he has depression and begins to attend Dr Bill as his guide.

STEP 2: He embarks on an eight-week holistic package of exercise, nutrition, supplements and ceasing alcohol. He also begins a course of antidepressants. By the end of this phase, he is feeling better.

STEP 3: From three to nine months, Paul does a lot of talk therapy while continuing with his holistic therapy regimen. He starts a long and difficult course of therapy to deal with his previous sexual abuse. He also does some CBT on his negative ruminations and unhelpful behavior.

STEP 4: From nine months onwards, he continues his antidepressants, consolidates his lifestyle changes, particularly exercise, and continues to work on his thinking and abusive past. After two years, he is off drug therapy, has disengaged from his therapist in relation to his abuse, and has taken up mindfulness to assist him with his negative ruminations. At present, four years after his suicide attempt, he continues to do well. He is even helping others who find themselves in similar difficulties.

## Mary's Story (revisited)

We met Mary on a number of occasions during the book. You may recall that she became depressed following a series of life events. Her sister's son took his own life and Mary ended up supporting her through this tragedy. Due to the recession, her workload increased. Her partner was placed on a three-day week and they ran into financial difficulties. She eventually took an overdose – and, fortunately, survived.

Mary ends up with Dr Bill. With the usual holistic package, including antidepressants, he manages to get her back to feeling better by eight weeks, and then begins the difficult task of helping her *get* better.

Firstly, they decide, together with her employers, that she will take time off work until she is feeling better and that she will continue her holistic therapy package. A financial expert assists her and her partner in restructuring their financial affairs.

She then begins to engage with talk therapy in order to deal with her negative ruminations, in particular her deep-seated belief that she is worthless.

By nine months, she is both feeling and getting better. She becomes anxious about ceasing antidepressants and Dr Bill ends up doing some CBT with her to help her deal with her anxiety in relation to depression relapse. She works hard and finds this concept, in her own words, 'awesome!'

From one year onwards, Mary is working hard to stay well. She has taken up yoga and is now working, on a voluntary basis, on a helpline dealing with depression. Three years later, Mary is still well.

## Dr Bill's Comments

Mary's story is a good example of the barrage of stressors that life sometimes throws at us – and that can spark a bout of major depression. She gets into difficulties when she has to assist her sister in dealing with the death of her nephew from suicide. But this is allied to the significant stressors of an increased workload, her partner going on to a three-day week, and her and her partner getting into serious financial difficulties.

Like some who get into difficulties with stress and a subsequent bout of severe depression, Mary responded with a suicide attempt. She survived, and was able to get assistance that allowed her to feel better within nine months. She required a full holistic package of lifestyle changes, financial advice, drug therapy and CBT to get better.

She has continued to stay well by continuing her lifestyle changes, yoga, and helping others in difficulties with depression through a helpline.

Mary's journey from near-death to mental health through our four-step process can be summarised as follows:

STEP 1: Mary ends up suffering from a series of stressors which trigger a bout of major depression and a serious suicide attempt. She survives, and ends up under the care of Dr Bill.

STEP 2: She works her way through an eight-week holistic package of exercise, nutrition, supplements, ceasing alcohol, taking antidepressants and reviewing the major stressors in her life. By the end of this phase, she is feeling better.

STEP 3: From three to nine months, she does a lot of talk therapy while continuing her holistic therapy regimen and meeting a financial advisor. She has now got better.

STEP 4: From nine months onwards, she ceases her antidepressants, consolidates lifestyle changes (particularly exercise), takes up yoga and continues to work on her thinking and her tendency to rate herself. She also does some CBT with Dr Bill to deal with her fears of relapsing if she ceases taking antidepressants.

## Claire's Story (revisited)

We met Claire much earlier in the book. She had suffered from anxiety since early childhood, like her father. She was a constant worrier and perfectionist.

By her mid-twenties, she had become quite successful. She met Tom, an easygoing teacher, and joins a company that recognises her dedicated perfectionist skills – and piles on the work! Then things began to take a turn for the worse. She finds her anxiety levels increasing and, for the first time in her life, develops panic attacks. It is no coincidence that the harder she tries to make sure everything at work is perfect, the more fatigue she develops.

Then comes the major shock: her mum is diagnosed with breast cancer. Claire's world starts to collapse. She had been sharing her problems with her mum, and that support has now gone. Tom is very sympathetic, but it isn't the same as talking to her mother. She becomes extremely stressed and anxious as her mum goes through the trauma of surgery and radiotherapy. Her mood plummets, she develops all the symptoms of major depression, and she begins to have panic attacks. Her employers try to make allowances for her reduced work output but eventually put pressure on her to seek assistance in the form of counselling – to little avail.

She starts losing weight, and takes little enjoyment in life. She begins to push Tom away, feeling that he could do a lot better than being with a worthless person like herself. Eventually she begins to have thoughts of self-harming; it is only the fact that her mum needs support from her that stops her from going down that road.

Luckily for Claire, her dad spots her drop in mood and sits her down for a chat. He tells her that he has had a number of bouts of depression over the years – most of which he handled on his own. He had always asked his wife to keep this fact away from his children, as he was ashamed of being seen to suffer from depression. Together they attend Dr Bill.

Dr Bill institutes a holistic package of lifestyle change and drug therapy, and enlists the support of Claire's employers. She doesn't want to begin drug therapy but Dr Bill explains the pros and cons of medication, and in the end she is happy to start. He also gives her CBT exercises for her panic attacks.

After eight weeks, she is feeling much better and is ready, with Dr Bill's assistance, to begin the next phase of her journey. This involves continuing the lifestyle changes and drug therapy, and beginning talk therapy, with a particular emphasis on her anxiety.

Dr Bill is pleased that, using the CBT exercises, she has come to terms with her acute anxiety and panic attacks. He takes the view that it is now time to use some further CBT to deal with her general anxiety.

He explains the 'ABC' system to her and they decide to do one on her mother's illness:

A:  Activating Event
- Trigger: Her mother's diagnosis of breast cancer
- Inference/danger: That her mother might not recover from her illness and would die

B:  Belief/Demand
- That her mother must not die; if this happened, she wouldn't be able to

cope and she would be a failure for letting it happen!

C: Consequences

- Emotion: Anxiety and low mood
- Physical Reactions: The usual symptoms of anxiety (stomach in knots, tension headache, palpitations, difficulties sleeping, difficulties breathing, and fatigue)
- Behaviour: Constantly ringing her mother and doctors to make sure that nothing is left to chance, stopping eating, misusing alcohol, ringing friends to look for reassurance, using the internet to seek the most up-to-date information on her mother's condition, difficulties eating and sleeping.

Dr Bill then challenged her behaviour and unhealthy belief and demands, using the 'big MACS' which we discussed earlier in the book, and looking at how they were contributing to her anxiety.

M He challenged her need for 100 percent certainty that her mother must not die. Although it would be preferable that she would survive, there were too many factors outside of her control (the aggressiveness of the breast cancer, how far it had spread, her mother's natural immunity, and so on). Was there anything in life that was 100 percent certain?

A He challenged her assumption that the worst would inevitably happen, when there was no clear evidence to back this up.

C He challenged her view that she would not be able to cope if her mum did die. Would she not cope because it would be in her own interests, and in the interests of those she loved, to do so?

S He challenged the concept that if her mum died, she would be a failure.

Over a number of months, through a series of 'ABC's, Dr Bill helped her challenge her demands for control in all aspects of her life. She began to realise that all her life she had been:

- making impossible demands on herself;
- catastrophising about the worst-case scenario without any proof to back it up;
- assuming that she would not be able to cope if she didn't achieve these demands;
- rating herself as being worthless as a person if she couldn't achieve the unachievable demands she had placed on herself.

After nine months, Claire has travelled a long way down the road to recovery . She is off drug therapy and paying careful attention to her lifestyle. Her panic attacks are gone and she has found that the CBT exercises are greatly reducing her general anxiety.

After a year, she is well and has taken up mindfulness and yoga; she finds both very helpful. She has gradually disengaged from Dr Bill and is now able to challenge her own thoughts and behaviour when she becomes anxious. Her mother made a good recovery from cancer. Moreover, Claire is no longer insisting on 100 percent certainty that her mother will not have a relapse of her cancer: she realises that this, like so much in life, is outside of her control.

Two years later, she remains well!

### Dr Bill's Comments

Claire is a classical example of how interlinked anxiety and depression can be. Many end up treating their depression but overlooking their underlying anxiety, which is putting so much pressure on their emotional brain. The majority can trace the origins of their anxiety back to childhood.

They learn to live their lives with the straitjacket of a constant demand for certainty and perfection. Since these are impossible demands for most of us at the best of times, it is no surprise that these people live their lives in a state of constant anxiety. In some cases, they may develop secondary panic attacks.

Claire was winning the battle for certainty and perfection during her childhood and adult life – but at a huge cost in terms of her general physical and mental health. But with her mother's illness, she encounters a situation which she cannot control and which she does not know how to handle. It is the stress of this (allied to underlying vulnerability) that leads her to develop major depression (for which she probably had a genetic predisposition, given that her father suffered from it).

She is the classical example of how the 'feel better, get better, stay well' approach works in action. She required the usual holistic package to feel better but needed a lot of CBT talk therapy to deal with her underlying anxiety in order to get better and to stay well for the future.

We can summarise Claire's journey from near-death to mental health through the four step process:

STEP 1: Claire, who has a long history of general anxiety, develops major depression as a result of her mum being diagnosed with breast cancer. With support from her father, she eventually goes to see Dr Bill for help.

STEP 2: She works her way through an eight-week holistic package of exercise, nutrition, supplements, ceasing alcohol, taking antidepressants and doing CBT exercises for her panic attacks. By the end of this phase, she is feeling better.

STEP 3: From three to nine months, she does a lot of talk therapy while continuing with her holistic therapy. In particular, she uses CBT exercises to deal with her general anxiety. She has now got better.

STEP 4: From nine months onwards, she stops taking antidepressants, consolidates lifestyle changes (particularly exercise) and takes up yoga and mindfulness. She continues to apply the CBT exercises to her life – with great effect. In particular, she accepts that she does not have to be perfect. She continues to be well.

## Peter's Story (revisited)

As you may recall, Peter was a man in his late thirties who experienced a bout of major depression when he was made redundant. He was filled with shame and guilt that he was unable to look after his family, and planned to take his own life. Thankfully, the intervention of his little daughter saved him, and he went to see Dr Bill. Following eight weeks of a holistic therapy package of exercise, nutrition, ceasing alcohol, taking supplements and following a course of drug therapy, Peter was feeling well enough to engage in talk therapy. Dr Bill helped him deal with his financial difficulties – his mortgage was subsequently restructured – and then examine retraining for the future.

Dr Bill then turned to Peter's negative thinking. When Peter was ready, they tackled the emotions that had nearly led to his demise: shame and guilt. Using some simple CBT concepts, Dr Bill assisted him in coming to terms with these.

After nine months, Peter has made giant progress. He is off drug therapy, and exercising regularly. He has done a number of courses and is actively considering starting his own business. He has also become involved in a local project, where he and others rent allotments; he has made new friends in the process. He takes up mindfulness, on the advice of Dr Bill, and finds it very helpful. He has also learned to value the extra time with his wife and children that being out of work for the year created. He spends two hours a week working on a helpline dedicated to helping those with depression: he gets a great deal of satisfaction from this work.

In particular, he has come to realise that he is much more than his job. He has also learned that looking after his physical and mental health is much more important than everything else. Three years later, he is running his own small export business and remains well. He often looks at his daughter and reflects on how close he came to ruining her life. What had started as a life crisis and ended up with depression was in the end managed by a number of small steps.

### Dr Bill's Comments

Peter's story is currently being replicated the length and breadth of Ireland, with many men and women finding themselves losing their jobs, ending up in financial difficulties and coming to be at risk of losing their homes. Many of them are deeply ashamed and guilty that they have (in their own minds) let down their families.

Some people who are already predisposed to major depression will succumb to the stress created by this situation. Sometimes the relationships within families also deteriorate, and this adds further stress. If major depression arrives, men in these situations are at high risk of suicidal thoughts and actions. This is especially so if shame and guilt are mixed with the depression, as is often the case.

Peter was lucky in that the emotional bond with his daughter triggered his emotional mind, and he came for help. Within eight weeks, he had responded well to the holistic package suggested by Dr Bill. But it was his systematic approach to his financial difficulties, his negative ruminations and his emotions of shame and guilt that allowed him to get better.

Peter has done a great deal to stay well. He has learned to continue his lifestyle changes, and has added mindfulness. He has also added a social dimension to his life, through becoming involved with the helpline and the allotment group. The fact that he has managed to set up his own business is perhaps the greatest testament to how well he has done.

He will always face the risk of further episodes of depression in the future, but he has managed to reduce greatly the risks of this occurring. Moreover, if it were to happen again, he would be much faster to seek help. We can summarise Peter's journey in our four-step process:

STEP 1: Following a series of major life stressors, Peter suffers a bout of major depression. With the help of his family, he realises that he needs some assistance, and decides to attend Dr Bill.

STEP 2: He embarks on an eight-week holistic package of exercise, nutrition, supplements and ceasing alcohol. He also begins a course of antidepressants. By the end of this phase, he is feeling better.

STEP 3: From three to nine months, Peter does a lot of talk therapy, while continuing his holistic therapy. He receives some financial advice and then engages in CBT exercises with Dr Bill to deal with his negative ruminations, shame and guilt.

STEP 4: By nine months, he is turning his attention to staying well. This involves a number of areas: setting up a new company, continuing his lifestyle changes (including exercise and mindfulness) and involvement in the community (the helpline and the allotment group). As a result of this combination, he remains well.

## Christina's Story (revisited)

Christina, a teacher in her mid-thirties, had a strong family history of depression, which affected her mother. You may remember that she was extremely traumatised by finding her mum almost dead following a major overdose of tablets. Christina had a history of recurrent depression and had attended a plethora of alternative and conventional therapists – to no avail. We meet her as she develops a bout of major depression following a period of stress at work.

She ends up attending Dr Bill and, after following his holistic approach of lifestyle changes (particularly exercise and ceasing alcohol) and a course of older antidepressants for eight weeks, feels much better. But she is still plagued by the constant internal ruminations in her mind, which told her she was worthless.

Dr Bill helps her deal with these negative thoughts using CBT concepts. He also sends her to a therapist to explore issues emanating from her childhood. As is sometimes the case, she hits a wall in relation to her struggle with the post-traumatic stress reaction she experienced after finding her mother so close to death.

Dr Bill reassures her that this is a classical example of a buried trauma from our past lurking in our emotional brain, giving rise to anxiety and, in some cases, triggering depression. By using simple CBT exercises, she comes to terms with her traumatic past.

After nine months, she is well, and ready to take on the next step – learning how to *stay* well. She is very nervous about coming off her antidepressants but with Dr Bill's assurance she does so. By one year, she has disengaged from both Dr Bill and her therapist.

She continues to exercise regularly and has become extremely aware of her alcohol intake. She has also taken up yoga and enjoys the physical and mental side of this discipline. She has become involved in a helpline dealing with depression.

Christina has learned to become much more realistic about the demands she makes on herself – and that she does not have to be perfect! She knows that she is likely to suffer a further bout of depression, based on her own and her family history, but knows that there is a great deal she can do to reduce the risk of this occurring.

Three years later, she remains well.

## Dr Bill's Comments

Christina comes from a household where depression was a constant companion to her parents. It is very common in such cases (due to a combination of genetic factors and the stress of growing up in such an environment) for the children to develop significant depression in their lives. A particular trigger for Christina was the trauma of seeing her mother almost die from a suicide attempt. This would have left a deep emotional scar, which she carried into her adult life.

She ended up trying to deal with her depression by using alternative therapy, and some conventional therapies. But none ever really reached the core problem of her buried trauma.

She also developed significant difficulties with negative rumination thoughts. It was critical that she felt better, through a holistic approach, before tackling these areas. In particular, she had to challenge her use of alcohol and to build exercise in to her daily routine.

She then had to do a lot of talk therapy to learn to deal with her negative thinking and post-traumatic symptoms. This is what really helped her turn the corner and stay well.

We can summarise her journey back to mental health through our four-step process:

STEP 1: Claire, who has a history of recurrent and familial depression, develops a bout following stress at work. On the advice of her principal, she ends up attending Dr Bill.

STEP 2: She works her way through an eight-week holistic package of exercise, nutrition, supplements, ceasing alcohol, taking antidepressants and doing CBT exercises for her panic attacks. By the end of this phase, she is feeling better.

STEP 3: From three to nine months, she does a lot of talk therapy while continuing with her holistic therapy. In particular, she learns new skills to help her deal with her negative thinking, including the trauma of her mum almost dying by suicide.

STEP 4: From nine months onwards, she ceases taking antidepressants, consolidates lifestyle changes (particularly exercise) and takes up yoga. She continues to apply the CBT anxiety exercises to her life – with great effect. She is staying well.

# YOUR JOURNEY ENDS

If you have stayed with us for the duration of your journey back to mental health, then well done! For many of you, it will have been a real struggle. The biggest hurdle may have come at Step One: accepting that you are depressed. If suicide thoughts are flooding your mind at this stage, it can be a real battle to look for help. Always remember all of the people who love you and who would be devastated if you travelled that particular road. The path I have laid out for you may be full of challenges, but will bring many rewards, both to yourself and to those you love. Some will have got through the second step, of feeling better, without any problem; others may have had a more difficult time. We are all different, and we must apply the whole holistic package to each individual. Some may need drug therapy and others may not. All will need a guide, empathy, and the determination to make the appropriate lifestyle changes. They will also need encouragement and support from family and friends in order to start feeling better.

For others, Step Three may provide the main stumbling block. Some may struggle with the negative ruminations that they are worthless, and so on. For others, the challenge may be trying to deal with major stress triggers in their lives. Still others may find the journey into dealing with emotions like anxiety, shame, guilt and hurt very traumatic and upsetting. But if they do not deal with them, they will find it very difficult to get better. In particular, anyone dealing with a background of abuse (especially sexual abuse) may struggle to come to terms with what occurred. For some, the pain and trauma is too great and they may disengage before real healing has taken place.

But it is critical that you deal with the issues mentioned. Otherwise, you may end up *feeling* better but not *getting* better. If you have gone through these three steps, then the real challenge is to stay well. Many get into trouble at this stage, turning their backs on the lifestyle changes which helped them so much – particularly in relation to exercise and alcohol.

For some, the problem may be the battle with the constant negative thoughts flowing through their emotional mind when depressed. In the case of the smaller number of people who end up needing maintenance drug therapy, the decision to stop the course may trigger a new episode. Finally, an inability to deal with some significant stressors in their lives may end up triggering a new episode.

However, it is my experience that those who have learned to deal with depression bouts in the above four-step manner seem to relapse rarely. Even if they do, they often recover quickly.

A key message is that although drug therapy can be an extremely useful adjunct to treating depression, nothing will ever replace empathy, lifestyle changes and talk therapy if we want to get better and stay well.

If you have fallen by the wayside in your journey, my advice is to retreat back to the previous step in the book and start again. Always do this with a professional guide such as a doctor or a trained therapist. They will accompany you on the journey. Remember, 'Two shortens the road!'

# APPENDIX

## What About Bipolar Disorder?

This is constantly confused with major depression by the public and the media alike. To deal with this subject fully is not within the remit of this book. For those who wish to read about the subject in more detail, see my first two books, *Flagging the Problem* and *Flagging the Therapy*. Here, I will summarise the key points of this condition.

Bipolar Disorder (sometimes called manic depression) is often confused with unipolar depression. In unipolar depression, mood can swing from normal to low, and back again, but does not become elevated. In bipolar, intermittent bouts of low, normal and elevated mood may be present.

Bipolar Disorder can be divided into two main groups:

### Bipolar Disorder, Type One

Here, the person will have suffered at least one manic episode, usually associated with some periods of low mood or depression. They suffer the usual symptoms of depression, which have already been dealt with, such as low mood, sleep difficulties, fatigue, low self-esteem, anxiety and suicidal thoughts.

Mania is the opposite of depression. It is defined as a distinct period of abnormally and persistently elevated mood which lasts at least one week, and sometimes requires hospitalisation. During the period of elevated mood, the person will display the following:

- extremely inflated self-esteem and mood

- decreased need for sleep
- talkativeness, and speech will often rhyme like poetry
- racing thoughts and ideas
- high creativity
- inexhaustible optimism
- energy and enthusiasm
- anger upon being challenged
- indiscreet behaviour, with very poor judgement
- insensitivity to the feelings of others
- impairment of social function, particularly in relation to everyday activities
- involvement in pleasurable activities with no regard for the consequences, such as spending sprees, shoplifting, reckless driving, excessive sexual activity, or impulsive behaviour.

A very unpleasant form of bipolar disorder, type one, is Dysphoric Mania. This is where the person gets a bout of depression during an episode of severe mania. Instead of feeling 'on top of the world', the person becomes extremely distressed, irritable and agitated, with racing and suicidal thoughts. This condition, which constitutes up to 30 to 40 percent of cases of mania, is more common in women. It is associated with a high suicide risk and a higher rate of familial depression, and will usually require hospitalisation. It can be a very distressing condition for both the person and their family. It can also be present in a lesser form as Dysphoric Hypomania, where depression is present during an episode of hypomania (see below).

## Bipolar Disorder, Type Two

Here, the person suffers mainly from bouts of depression, interspersed with periods of hypomania. Hypomania is a distinct period of euphoria which lasts at least four days. During this period of elevated mood, the symptoms of mania emerge. However, these symptoms are not as obvious as in Type One Bipolar Disorder, usually do not cause major difficulties for the person when it comes to coping with normal activities (in fact, many feel that they cope better during the period of elevated mood) and seldom lead to the person requiring hospitalisation. The individual will rarely suffer from delusions or hallucinations. A person with hypomania will have periods where they experience the following:

- a sudden increase in energy levels
- racing thoughts
- increased talkativeness
- a decreased need for sleep
- irritability and annoyance if confronted
- feeling on top of the world

In future, there may also be a third type of Bipolar Disorder – namely antidepressant triggered bipolar disorder, where latent illness is unmasked by the antidepressants.

Bipolar disorder sometimes appears in the teenage years, and even when observed, is often misdiagnosed as normal depression. Only when the elevated mood periods are either admitted to or noticed by others does the real diagnosis emerge. Bouts of low mood, periods of normality and occasional bouts of elevated mood merge to create the distinct pattern of this illness. Unfortunately, there is often a significant delay in diagnosis, due to the erratic nature of the illness. Some people may (through a combination of not presenting early enough and a delay in accurate diagnosis) remain undetected for up to ten years. Only one in four bipolar depressives are diagnosed within three years of onset of the condition.

Over their lifetime, a bipolar sufferer will experience eight to ten episodes of mood swings. Untreated episodes of mania may last from four to six months. Mania symptoms are generally so severe that help is usually received quite quickly, so episodes may last only weeks. Episodes of hypomania are much more subtle and are of shorter duration; as a result, they often go undetected. Bouts of depression may, if left untreated, last for up to nine months. One of the difficulties with biplar disorder is that patients who are treated with antidepressants may develop a subsequent bout of hypomania or mania as a result of the medication. A particular concern is where a person with dysphoric hypomania presents with what may appear at first glance to be simple depression, and is treated with antidepressants. This can make them more agitated, and suicide thoughts and actions may increase.

The risk of suicide in general in bipolar disorder is highest in the early stages of the illness (which is why early diagnosis is vital) and occurs more often in the depression or mixed-mania phases than in other phases. There can be a delay of four to five years between the first and second episodes. Following this, the length of time between episodes will gradually reduce. In some cases, the severity of the illness, especially if it is left untreated, will worsen. Some estimate the probability of recurrence at 50 percent for the first year, 70 percent by the fourth year and 90 percent by the fifth year.

Bipolar depression is not as common as unipolar depression, and affects men and women equally. The incidence of bipolar type one is 1 percent, and bipolar type two between 1 and 2 percent. Some experts believe that the true incidence of type two may be considerably higher.

Bipolar disorder is best treated by mood stabilisers rather than antidepressants, combined with the lifestyle changes and talk therapies discussed earlier. Mood stabilisers (many of which were originally developed as anti-epilepsy drugs) work by stabilising the internal chemistry of the brain cells involved, and have transformed the lives of many sufferers. Drugs like Lithium and Epilim are very useful in situations where the predominant issue is elevated mood, and others, like Lamictal, are prescribed where mood is depressed. Mood stabilisers have side effects. Lithium and Epilim both cause weight gain and should be avoided in pregnancy; Lithium can also cause tremors. Lamictal can cause rashes. Finally, antipsychotic drugs like Zyprexa and Seroquel are used by some psychiatrists as long-term mood stabilisers for the management of elevated mood.

# BIBLIOGRAPHY

Barry, H. P., (2013). Identifying cognitive symptoms in depression in primary care. THINC Expert Forum Berlin.

Barry, H. P. (2007). Flagging the problem: a new approach to mental health. Dublin: Liberties Press.

Barry, H. P. (2013). Flagging the therapy: pathways out of depression and anxiety. Dublin: Liberties Press.

Barry, H. P. (2010). Flagging stress: toxic stress and how to avoid it. Dublin: Liberties Press.

Beck, A.T., Rush, A.J., Shaw, B.F., et al. Cognitive therapy of depression. Guilford Press; 1979

Beck, A. T., & Dozois, D. J. (2013). Cognitive Therapy: Current Status and Future Directions. Annual Review of Medicine Vol. 62: 397-409

Beck, A.T., The current state of cognitive therapy: a 40-year retrospective. 2005. Arch Gen Psychiatry. 62(9):953-959.

Blashki, G., Richards, J. C., Ryan, P., Pierce, D., McCabe, M., Morgan, H., Hickie, I.B. & Sumich, H. 2003, Cognitive behavioural strategies for general practice. Australian family physician, 32: 11, 910-917.

Christensen, H., Griffin, K.M., & Jorm, A. F. 2004 Delivering interventions for depression by using the internet: randomized controlled trial. British Medical Journal 328, 7434, 265

Conradi, H.J., Ormel, J., & and de Jonge, P. 2011. Presence of individual (residual) symptoms during depressive episodes and periods of remission: a 3-year prospective study. Psychol Med 2011; 41: 1165-11742

Cujipers, P., van Straten, A., Hollon, S.D., et al. The contribution of active medication to combined treatments of psychotherapy and pharmacotherapy for adult depression: a meta-analysis. Acta Psychiatr Scand 2010;121:415-23.

Davidson, A.S., Fosgerau, C.F., What is depression? 2014. Psychiatrists' and GPs' experiences of diagnosis and the diagnostic process. International Journal of Qualitative Studies on Health and Well-being 2014; 9:24866

David, L. 2006. Using CBT in General Practice. The 10 Minute Consultation. Scion Publications.

David, L., & Freeman, G. 2006. Cognitive Behavioural Model (CBM). Education for Primary Care 17; 443 – 53)

Drevets, W. C. (2007), 'Orbitofrontal cortex function and structure in depression', Annals of the New York Academy of Sciences, 1121 (1), 499-527. (2001), 'Neuroimaging and neuropathological studies of depression: Implications for the cognitive-emotional features of mood disorders', Current Opinion in Neurobiology, 11, 240-49. (2000), 'Neuroimaging of mood disorders', Biological Psychiatry, 48, 813-29. (1999), 'Prefrontal cortical-amygdalar metabolism in major depression', Annals of the New York Academy of Sciences, 877, 614-37

Dryden, W., Ellis, A. 2001. Rational emotive behaviour therapy. Handbook of cognitive-behavioral therapies. 2nd ed. New York: Guilford Press.

Dryden, W., Neenam, M. 2004. Rational Emotive Behavioural Counselling in Action. Sage Publications. London

Ellis, A. 1962. Reason and Emotion in Psychotherapy. New York: Lyle Stuart.

Ellis, A. 1996. Better, Deeper and More Enduring Brief Therapy. The Rational Emotive Behaviour Therapy Approach. Brunner/Mazel, Inc. New York.

Freedy, J.R., Carek, P. J., Diaz, V. A., & Thiedke, C.C. 2012. Integrating Cognitive Behavioural Therapy into the Management of Depression. American Family Physician April 1, 2012 Volume 85, Number 7

Goldapple, K., Segal, Z., Garson, C., Lau, M., Bieling, P., Kennedy, S., & Maynerg H. 2004. Modulation of cortical-limbic pathways in major depression: treatment-specific effects of cognitive behaviour therapy. Arch Gen Psychiatry: 61(1):34–41.

Hammar, Å., Årdal, G. 2009. Cognitive functioning in major depression – a summary. Front Hum Neurosci ; 3:26.

Harmer, C. J., Goodwin, G. M. & Cowen, P. J. 2009. Why do antidepressants take so long to work? A cognitive neuropsychological model of antidepressant drug action. The British Journal of Psychiatry, 195, 102-8.

Holford, P. (2003), Optimum Nutrition for the Mind, London: Judy Piaktus Ltd

Kandel, E. R. and L. R. Squire (2001), 'Neuroscience: Breaking down scientific barriers to the study of brain and mind', Annals of the New York Academy of Sciences, 935 (1), 118-35

Kessler, D., Lewis, G., Kaur, S., Wiles, N., King, M., Weich, S., Sharp, D. J, Araya, R., Hollinghurst, S., & Peters, T.J. 2009. Therapist-delivered internet psychotherapy for depression in primary care: a randomised controlled trial. Lancet 2009; 374: 628–34

King, M., Davidson, O., Taylor, F., Haines, A., Sharp, D., & Turner, R. (2002). Effectiveness of teaching general practitioners skills in brief cognitive behavioural therapy to treat patients with depression: randomised controlled trial. BMJ. Vol: 324, 7343.

Kukyken, W., Dalgleish, T., & Holden, E. R. 2007. Advances in Cognitive-Behavioural Therapy for Unipolar Depression. Can J Psychiatry 2007; 52:5–13.

Lam, R.W. Depression, 2nd Edition, Revised. Oxford University Press, 2012

Logan, A. C. (2004), 'Omega-3 fatty acids and major depression: A primer for the mental health professional', Lipids in Health and Disease, 3(1), 25

Mayberg, H. S. (2003), 'Modulating dysfunctional limbic-cortical circuits in depression: Towards development of brain-based algorithms for diagnosis and optimised treatment', British Medical Bulletin, 65, 193-207. (2005), 'Deep brain stimulation for treatment resistant depression', Neuron, 45 (5), 651-60

Murphy, E. (2009), 'The raggy doll club', Forum

Murphy, E. (2013). Five steps to happiness. Dublin: Liberties Press

Ochsner, K. N., R. D. Ray, J. C. Cooper, E. R. Robertson, S. Chopra, J. D. Gabrieli and J. J. Gross (2004), 'For better or for worse: neural systems supporting the cognitive down- and up-regulation of negative emotion', Neuroimage, 23 (2), 483-99

Raison, C. L. (2008), 'Buddhists meet mind scientist in conference on meditation and depression', Psychiatric Times, 25 (3)

Rock, P. L., Roiser, J. P., Riedel, W. J. & Blackwell, A. D. 2013. Cognitive impairment in depression: a systematic review and meta-analysis. Psychol Med, 1-12.

Roiser, J.P., Sahakian, B.J. (2013). Hot and cold cognition in depression. CNS Spectr 2013; 18:139-49

Roiser, J.P., Elliot, R., & Sahakian, B.J. 2012. Cognitive Mechanisms of Treatment in Depression. Neuropsychopharmacology REVIEWS: 37, 117–136.

Russo-Neustadt, A. A., R. C. Beard, Y. M. Huang and C. W. Cotman (2000), 'Physical activity and antidepressant treatment potentiate the expression of specific brain-derived neurotrophic factor transcripts in the rat hippocampus', Neuroscience, 101 (2), 305-12

Schuch, F.B., et al. 2015. Exercise as a treatment for depression: a meta – analysis adjusting for publication bias. Journal of Psychiatric Research 77: 42 -51

Segal, Z.V., Williams, M.G., Teasdale, J.D. 2002. Mindfulness-based cognitive therapy for depression: a new approach to preventing relapse. Guilford Press, 2002.

Sipe, W.E., Eisendrath, S.J. 2012. Mindfulness-based cognitive therapy: theory and practice. Can J Psychiatry. 57(2):63-9.

Spek, V., Cujipers, P., NPyklicep, I., Riper, H., & Keyzer, J. 2007. Internet-based cognitive behaviour therapy for symptoms of depression and anxiety: a meta-analysis. Pop Psychol Med. 37(3):319-28.

Thase, M. E., Kingdon, D., Turkington, D. The promise of cognitive behaviour therapy for treatment of severe mental disorders: a review of recent developments. World Psychiatry 2014; 13:244–250

Teasdale, J. D., Segal, Z. V., Williams, J. M. G., Ridgeway, V., Soulsby, J., & Lau, M. (2000). Prevention of relapse/recurrence in major depression by mindfulness-based cognitive therapy. Journal of Consulting and Clinical Psychology, 68, 615–623.

World Health Organisation. 2008. The global burden of disease: 2004 update.

Wiles, N., Thomas, L., Abel, A., Ridgeway, N., Turner, N., Cambell, J., Garland, A., Hollinghurst, S., Jerrom, B., Kessler, D., Kuyken, W., Morrison, J.,

Turner, K., Williams, C., Peters, T., & Lewis, G. 2013. Cognitive behavioural therapy as an adjunct to pharmacotherapy for primary care based patients with treatment resistant depression: results of the CoBalT randomised controlled trial. Lancet 2013; 381: 375–84

Williams, A. D., & Andrews, G. 2013. The Effectiveness of Internet Cognitive Behavioural Therapy (iCBT) for Depression in Primary Care: A Quality Assurance Study. PLoS ONE 8(2)

Zaretsky, A., Segal, Z., & Fefergrad, M. New Developments in Cognitive-Behavioural Therapy for Mood Disorders. Can J Psychiatry 52:3–4)

# DRUGS AND THERAPIES COMMONLY USED IN DEPRESSION

## Common Antidepressant Drugs in Use
*Drugs Which Affect The Serotonin Cable*

- Fluoxetine (Prozac, Prozamel, Gerozac)
- Citalopram (Cipramil, Citrol, Ciprager)
- Escitalopram (Lexapro)
- Paroxetine (Seroxat, Meloxat, Parox)
- Sertraline (Lustral) – this has minor effects on the dopamine cable as well

*Possible main side effects of these drugs*

- Initial nausea in first week in some cases
- Reduced libido and delayed orgasm in some cases
- Slightly heavier periods in some women
- Occasional mild tremors
- Initial fatigue and anxiety in certain cases

*Drugs Which Affect The Noradrenalin Cable*
- Reboxetine (Edronax)
- Possible main side effects of this drug
- Sweating, headaches and nausea
- Sleep difficulties
- Dry mouth
- Impotence in some cases

*Drugs Which Affect The Serotonin And Noradrenalin Cable*
- Venlafaxine (Effexor xL)
- Cymbalta (Duloxetine)
- Zispin (Mirtazapine)
- Possible main side effects of these drugs
- A mixture of both of the above groups of symptoms
- In the case of Mirtazapine: weight gain

## Older Antidepressants In Use
- Amitriptyline
- Trazodone (Molipaxin)
- Tofranil (Imipramine)
- Trimipramine (Surmontil)
- Lofepramine (Gamanil)
- Dothiepin (Prothiaden)

*Main side effects of these drugs*
- Drowsiness (apart from Imipramine)
- Higher risk of serious consequences if taken in overdose
- Dry mouth, constipation and blurred vision are quite common

*The Mood Stabilisers*
- Lithium (Priadel or Camcolit)
- Lamotrigine (Lamictal)
- Sodium valproate (Epilim)
- Carbamazepine (Tegretol)

*Main side effects of these drugs*
- Weight gain (particularly Lithium and Sodium Valproate)
- Skin rashes (particularly Lamotrigine)
- Teratogenic (all bar Lamotrigine)
- Dangerous in overdose (particularly Lithium)

*Drugs Which Affect The Melatonin System*
- Agomelatine (valdoxan)

*Possible side effects of this drug*
- No major side effects but liver function tests are advised

*Drugs Which Are Multimodal (Affecting Serotonin Cable And Other Receptors)*
- Vortioxetine (Brintellix)

*Possible side effects of this drug*
- nausea

*Major Tranquillisers (Also Known As Atypical Antipsychotics)*
- Olanzapine (Zyprexa)
- Quetiapine (Seroquel)
- Risperdal (Risperidone)
- Aripiprazole (Abilify)

*Possible main side effects of these drugs*
- Weight gain (particularly Olanzapine)
- Increased risks of Insulin Resistance and Diabetes
- Potential risks of Metabolic Syndrome and Coronary Heart Disease

## Common Anti-Anxiety Drugs In Use

### The Benzodiazepines: Long-Acting
- Diazepam (Valium)
- Chlordiazepoxide (Librium)
- Clonazepam (Rivotril)

### The Benzodiazepines: Short-To Medium-Acting
- Bromazepam (Lexotane)
- Alprazolam (Xanax, Gerax)

*Possible main side effects of Benzodiazepines*
- Drowsiness
- Impairment of concentration
- High risk of becoming dependent if used for long periods

- High risk of developing tolerance to these drugs

PREGBALIN (LYRICA)
*Possible side effects of this drug*
- Dizziness and coordination difficulties
- Drowsiness
- Weight gain
- Dry mouth
- Headaches

## Antidepressants In Pregnancy

Should be used only if significant depression is present and other therapies are not sufficient.

There is no evidence that modern SSRIs (apart fromParoxetine) are teratogenic. I recommend using the minimal dose necessary and withdrawing it at thirty-eight weeks (to restart after baby is born if required) to reduce any withdrawal symptoms in the newborn baby. There must be full consultation with and information given to mother (and father) before any course is started – the mother must be happy to proceed. There is evidence of greater incidence of low birth weight and prematurity in babies born to both those treated with antidepressants and those born to mothers with untreated depression. Treating the mother may reduce the risks of potential suicide and possibility of serious postnatal depression affecting both mother and newborn baby. Using an antidepressant in pregnancy does not mean you are somehow inferior or 'putting your baby at risk', it may at times be more damaging in some situations not to use them. If in doubt, have a chat with your family doctor and if necessary seek a specialist psychiatric opinion.

## Antidepressants In Breastfeeding

Amounts of modern SSRIs found in breast milk are quite small. Postnatal depression if severe may require use of an antidepressant if other therapies not sufficient. There is no evidence that usage of these drugs in the postnatal period has any adverse effects on babies.

I personally am quite comfortable with using them, if required. Treatment of postnatal depression may reduce risk of suicide.

## Light Therapies For SAD

Light box/lamp of at least 10,000 lux is considered standard. Some feel the blue wavelength part of the light spectrum is the most effective. It requires thirty minutes of therapy per day at 10,000 lux. Morning is much better than evening.

Ideally combine this with use of a dawn simulator set to come on an hour before rising in the winter months. Some do well with simple dawn simulator (250 – 400 lux). Dawn simulators are also ideal for many who get simple winter blues but do not suffer from depression or SAD.

Two useful contact details of suppliers:

*www.brighterday.ie*
*www.sad.co.uk*

# SELF-HELP GROUPS

## Alcoholics Anonymous

Alcoholics Anonymous 'AA' is an international organisation with over 2,000,000 members who have recovered from or are suffering from alcohol abuse or addiction. AA is concerned solely with the personal recovery and continued sobriety of individual alcoholics; it does not engage in the fields of alcoholism research, medical or psychiatric treatment, education, or advocacy in any form but provides peer-to-peer support within a Fellowship structure. There are approximately 4,400 group meetings each week throughout Great Britain. The AA is fully self-supporting and does not accept donations from non-members. All contributions are voluntary.

Helpline: 0800 917 7650
help@aamail.org | www.alcoholics-anonymous.org.uk

## Anxiety UK

Anxiety UK is a national registered charity formed in 1970 to provide help for anyone affected by anxiety, stress and anxiety based depression. The website maintains an up to date list of independent, verified self help groups located across the UK and provides a wealth of self help resources online.
Helpline: 08444 755 744
support@anxietyuk.org.uk | www.anxietyuk.org.uk

## Aware

Aware is a voluntary organisation established in 1985 to support those experiencing depression and their families. Aware endeavours to create a society where people with mood disorders and their families are understood and supported, and to obtain the resources to enable them to defeat depression. Weekly support group meetings at approximately fifty locations nationwide, including Northern Ireland, offer peer support and provide factual information, and enable people to gain the skills they need to help them cope with depression. Aware's 'Beat the Blues' educational programme is run in secondary schools.

Helpline: 1890 303 302 (Ireland only)
support@aware.ie | www.aware.ie | 01 661 7211

## ChildLine

ChildLine, a service run by the ISPCC, seeks to empower and support children using the medium of telecommunications and information technology. The service is designed for all children and young people up to the age of eighteen in Ireland.

Helpline: 0800 1111

## Grow

Established in Ireland in 1969, GROW is Ireland's largest mutual-help organisation in the area of mental health. It is anonymous, nondenominational, confidential and free. No referrals are necessary. GROW aims to achieve self-activation through mutual help. Its members are enabled, over time, to craft a step-by-step recovery or personal-growth plan, and to develop leadership skills that will help others.

Helpline: 1 890 474 474 (Ireland only)
info@grow.ie | www.grow.ie

# Mind

Mind is one of the UK's leading mental health charities. The organisation has been committed to making sure that mental health advice and support is accessible for anyone who needs it. In 2013 the charity successfully campaigned against the Mental Health (Discrimination) Act, removing the last significant forms of discrimination that prevented people with mental health problems from serving on a jury, being a director of a company or serving as an MP. With over 375,000 local Minds across England and Wales, the charity provides millions with services that include supported housing, crisis helplines, drop-in centres, employment and training schemes, counselling, peer support, information and befriending.

Helpline: 0300 123 3393

info@mind.org.uk | www.mind.org.uk

# No Panic

No Panic is a charity which aims to facilitate the relief and rehabilitation of people suffering from panic attacks, phobias, obsessive compulsive disorders and other related anxiety disorders, including tranquilliser withdrawal, and to provide support to sufferers and their families and carers. Founded by Colin M. Hammond in the UK, this group has extended its activities to Ireland, where it is organised by therapist Caroline McGuigan.

Helpline: 0 844 967 4848
Youth Helpline: 0 175 384 0393
admin@nopanic.org.uk | nopanic.org.uk | 0 195 268 0460

## Samaritans

Samaritans was started in 1953 in London by a young vicar called Chad Varah; the first branch in the Republic of Ireland opened in Dublin in 1970. Samaritans provides a twenty-four-hour-a-day confidential service offering emotional support for people who are experiencing feelings of distress or despair, including those which may lead to suicide.

Helpline: 116 123
jo@samaritans.org | www.samaritans.org

## Sane

Established in 1986 to improve the quality of life for all those affected by mental health problems, SANE is a UK-wide charity with three main objectives: to raise awareness and combat stigma about mental illness; to provide emotional support and care; to aid research into the causes and treatments of serious mental health conditions such as schizophrenia and depression. SANE provides confidential emotional support, information and access to self-management strategies.

Helpline: 0300 304 7000
info@sane.org.uk | www.sane.org.uk

# ACKNOWLEDGEMENTS

I would like to start by thanking my editorial team in Orion for all their wonderful assistance in republishing this book. In particular, I want to thank Olivia Morris who has believed in the *Flag* series from the beginning and who has been so supportive. I also owe a huge debt of gratitude to Vanessa Fox O' Loughlin and Dominic Perrim my two agents who have made all of this possible.

I would also like to thank my dear friend and colleague Dr Muiris Houston for taking the time to review the text, and for his friendship and support. His reports in the excellent *Irish Times* Health Plus supplement are respected by us all. And I include a special word of thanks to Carol Hunt of the *Sunday Independent* for her kind review and constant support. We are lucky to have journalists of this quality in Ireland. I would also like to say 'thank you' to Maria Carmody for taking time out of her busy schedule to review the text. I send the warmest thanks to Cathy Kelly (best-selling author and UNICEF ambassador) for her constant kindness and support throughout the years. I am, as always, indebted to my friend and colleague Enda Murphy (and his wife Mei), for his invaluable assistance. We both value our national radio slot with the Sean O' Rourke show very highly and I would like to take this opportunity to thank Sean and his wonderful team for allowing us to highlight key areas of mental health.

I would like to say a special thanks to my colleague Professor Catherine Harmer (Professor of Cognitive Neuroscience, University of Oxford) who took some time out of her very busy schedule to review this book. My special thanks also to friends and colleagues Professor Raymond Lam (Professor of Mood and

# Also by
# DR HARRY BARRY

**TOXIC STRESS**

A step-by-step guide
to managing stress

DR HARRY BARRY

**ANXIETY AND PANIC**

How to reshape your
anxious mind and brain

DR HARRY BARRY

**DEPRESSION**

A practical guide

DR HARRY BARRY

**FLAGGING THE THERAPY**

Pathways out of
depression and anxiety

DR HARRY BARRY

**FLAGGING THE PROBLEM**

A new approach to
mental health

DR HARRY BARRY

S